633.8
HUG
CPS – MORRILL SCHOOL
Flavor foods.
34880030010644
W9-BBN-003

PROPERTY OF
CHICAGO BOARD OF EDUCATION
DONALD L. MORRILL SCHOOL

Saffron
Pepper
Vanilla
Basil
Rosemary
Parsley

PLANTS WE EAT

Cinnamon
Cassia
Ginger
Horseradish
Licorice
Turmeric
Mustard
Nutmeg
Mace
Cloves
Saffron
Pepper
Vanilla

Flavor Foods

Spices & Herbs

Meredith Sayles Hughes

Lerner Publications Company/Minneapolis

Check out the author's website at www.foodmuseum.com/hughes

Lerner Publications Company
A Division of Lerner Publishing Group
241 First Avenue North
Minneapolis, MN 55401 U.S.A.

Website address: www.lernerbooks.com

Designer: Steven P. Foley
Editor: Amy M. Boland
Photo Researcher: Glenn Marier

LIBRARY OF CONGRESS CATALOGING-IN-PUBLICATION DATA

Hughes, Meredith Sayles
Flavor foods: spices & herbs / by Meredith Sayles Hughes.
p. cm. — (Plants we eat)
Includes index.
Summary: Describes the historical origins, uses, and growing requirements of various spices and herbs, such as pepper, vanilla, nutmeg, horseradish, licorice, and ginger. Includes recipes.
ISBN 0–8225–2835–5 (lib. bdg. : alk. paper)
1. Spice plants — Juvenile literature. 2. Spices — Juvenile literature. 3. Herbs — Juvenile literature. 4. Cookery (Spices) — Juvenile literature. 5. Cookery (Herbs) — Juvenile literature. [1. Spices. 2. Herbs.] I. Title. II. Series: Hughes, Meredith Sayles. Plants we eat.
SB305.H84 1999
633.8'3—dc21 99–18757

Manufactured in the United States of America.
1 2 3 4 5 6 – JR – 05 04 03 02 01 00

The glossary on page 85 gives definitions of words shown in **bold type** in the text.

Contents

Introduction

Plants make all life on our planet possible. They provide the oxygen we breathe and the food we eat. Think about a burger and fries. The meat comes from cattle, which eat plants. The fries are potatoes cooked in oil from soybeans, corn, or sunflowers. The burger bun is a wheat product. Ketchup is a mixture of tomatoes, herbs, and corn syrup or the sugar from sugarcane. How about some onions or pickle relish with your burger?

First we eat, then we do everything else.

—M. F. K. Fisher

How Plants Make Food

By snatching sunlight, water, and carbon dioxide from the atmosphere and mixing them together—a complex process called **photosynthesis**—green plants create food energy. The raw food energy is called glucose, a simple form of sugar. From this storehouse of glucose, each plant produces fats, carbohydrates, and proteins—the elements that make up the bulk of the foods humans and animals eat.

Sunlight peeks through the branches of a plant-covered tree in a tropical rain forest, where all the elements exist for photosynthesis to take place.

Plants offer more than just food. They provide the raw materials for making the clothes you're wearing and the paper in books, magazines, and newspapers. Much of what's in your home comes from plants—the furniture, the wallpaper, and even the glue that holds the paper on the wall. Eons ago plants created the gas and oil we put in our cars, buses, and airplanes. Plants even give us the gum we chew.

On the Move

Organisms that behave like algae—small, rootless plants that live in water

Although we don't think of plants as beings on the move, they have always been pioneers. From their beginnings as algaelike creatures in the sea to their movement onto dry land about 400 million years ago, plants have colonized new territories. Alone on the barren rock of the earliest earth, plants slowly established an environment so rich with food, shelter, and oxygen that some forms of marine life took up residence on dry land. Helped along by birds who scattered seeds far and wide, plants later sped up their travels, moving to cover most of our planet.

Early in human history, when few people lived on the earth, gathering food was everyone's main activity. Small family groups were nomadic, venturing into areas that offered a source of water, shelter, and foods such as fruits, nuts, seeds, and small game animals. After they had eaten up the region's food sources, the family group moved on to another spot. Only when people noticed that food plants were renewable—that the berry bushes would bear fruit again and that grasses gave forth seeds year after year—did family groups begin to settle in any one area for more than a single season.

It's a Fact!

The term *photosynthesis* comes from Greek words meaning "putting together with light." This chemical process, which takes place in a plant's leaves, is part of the natural cycle that balances the earth's store of carbon dioxide and oxygen.

Native Americans were the first peoples to plant crops in the Americas.

Domestication of plants probably began as an accident. Seeds from a wild plant eaten at dinner were tossed onto a trash pile. Later a plant grew there, was eaten, and its seeds were tossed onto the pile. The cycle continued on its own until someone noticed the pattern and repeated it deliberately. Agriculture radically changed human life. From relatively small plots of land, more people could be fed over time, and fewer people were required to hunt and gather food. Diets shifted from a broad range of wild foods to a more limited but more consistent menu built around one main crop such as wheat, corn, cassava, rice, or potatoes. With a stable food supply, the world's population increased and communities grew larger. People had more time on their hands, so they turned to refining their skills at making tools and shelter and to developing writing, pottery, and other crafts.

Plants We Eat

This series examines the wide range of plants people around the world have chosen to eat. You will discover where plants came from, how they were first grown, how they traveled from their original homes, and where they have become important and why. Along the way, each book looks at the impact of certain plants on society and discusses the ways in which these food plants are sown, harvested, processed, and sold. You will also discover that some plants are key characters in exciting high-tech stories. And there are plenty of opportunities to test recipes and to dig into other hands-on activities.

The series Plants We Eat divides food plants into a variety of informal categories. Some plants are prized for their seeds, others for their fruits, and some for their underground roots, tubers, or bulbs. Many plants offer leaves or stalks for good eating. Humans convert some plants into oils and others into beverages or flavorings. Spices are the dried plant parts, and herbs are the fresh or dried leaves, that season our foods. People have added flavorful plants to their food ever since the first person discovered that cooked meat went down more easily (and tasted better) than raw meat. Long before recorded history, hunters provided meat that could be quickly eaten on the spot or simply smoked and dried for future use. At least 10,000 years ago, people domesticated animals, and meat became far more plentiful than it had ever been before. Seasonings began to play a larger role in making foodstuffs taste better. People could use flavorings to help cure meats—that is, to preserve them for a while—or to make spoiled meat more palatable.

A wide variety of spices has flavored people's food since ancient times.

For centuries salt was the key tool for preserving meat. Salt is not a spice at all, but a mineral. Before

people had refrigerators, they could keep food from spoiling by pickling it in a solution of vinegar and salt or by packing dried foods in salt. The result was, of course, salty food that all began to taste much the same. People wanted to liven up their food with new flavorings, and spices did the trick.

Some of the plants in *Flavor Foods: Spices & Herbs*—such as mustard, licorice, horseradish, and most of the common herbs—originated in the world's **temperate zones.** But many others grow only in the **tropics.** Some grew only on certain little-known islands. Spices from tropical Asia—specifically, from the modern-day countries of China, Malaysia, India, Sri Lanka, and especially Indonesia—inspired crucial events in world history. Although the spice story affected people all over the world, Europeans were the main characters. In their minds, tropical spices were prestigious and valuable. Throughout the ages, European demand for these flavorings sparked profitable trade empires, greed and exploitation, warfare and political domination. An understanding of this history is crucial to understanding the tales of the individual herbs and spices in *Flavor Foods.*

Early Times

At some time, Southeast Asians may have been the only ones to enjoy the spices that grew in their area of the world. But for thousands of years, these people have been exporting spices to their neighbors. Perhaps even earlier than 2600 B.C., Egyptian rulers fed spices to the workers who built their pyramids. The ancient Chinese enjoyed spices, and Europeans used foreign flavorings well before the founding of Rome in 753 B.C.

In this Roman carving, one servant *(left)* grinds spices in a wealthy family's kitchen while another slices meat *(right)*.

Merchants probably transported spices along routes within Southeast Asia, then shipped them to East Africa, the Arabian Peninsula, northern China, and the Mediterranean.

For centuries Arabs from the Middle East controlled the spice trade with Europe, carrying cargoes in small boats with triangular sails. In ancient times, sea travel was dangerous. Most of the world was poorly mapped, if charted at all. Aboard a ship at sea, there was no way to communicate with people on land and only the sun and stars by which to navigate. Sometimes the entire ship, complete with crew and cargo, got lost and never returned home. Because of the high risks of sea travel, foreign goods were very expensive—and the more exotic and scarce the items, the more costly they were. The Arabs kept their spice routes secret from their customers so they could maintain a monopoly on—that is, they could be the only suppliers of—the valuable flavorings. European demand for spices rose as the Romans began to build their empire in the 200s B.C.

When in Rome

Wealthy citizens of the Roman Empire (27 B.C. to A.D 476) led an extravagant lifestyle. They loved anything costly or exotic, and spices suited them to a T—far more so than the flavorful, but ordinary, temperate seasonings that grew wild in Europe and were free for the picking. Spices poured into the Roman port of Alexandria, Egypt. Traders from Southeast Asia came via the Persian Gulf (an arm of the Indian Ocean) and merchants traveled from China by way of an overland route called the Silk Road. Roman vessels eventually made their way from Egypt south through the Red Sea and east across the Indian Ocean to India, the source of many spices. But the two-year trip was grueling, so Rome was largely at the mercy of foreign spice merchants until around 50 B.C. At that time, the neighboring Greeks discovered how to sail to India on the monsoon winds, which blow east for six months and west for six months. In the summer, Roman ships could travel to India. They could return to the Mediterranean in winter with the west winds. By making the trip themselves, Roman merchants could earn bigger spice profits, since they wouldn't have to pay the higher price the Arabs charged.

The Crusades

In the A.D. 400s, the Roman Empire had grown too big to manage and defend. In 476 it collapsed, bringing down major trade networks with it. Europeans forgot the cooking lore of the Roman upper set, and few could afford pricey spices, anyway. The seagoing merchants of Venice, then an independent Italian city-state, jumped into the spice game by sailing to Alexandria, where they could still pick up cargoes that Arabs brought from afar. In the 600s, an Arab religious leader named Muhammad founded the faith of Islam, which spread quickly throughout the Middle East. Followers of Islam, called Muslims, expanded their ranks by conquest. Their empire grew to encompass a

It's a Fact!

Muhammad, the founder of Islam, was a camel driver who married the widow of a wealthy Arab spice trader in 595.

Marco Polo, Phone Home!

Marco Polo was the son of a wealthy jewel merchant from Venice. In 1271, when young Marco was only 17, he accompanied his father and uncle on a lengthy trip to China. The Polos spent 17 years traveling throughout modern-day China, India, Myanmar, Laos, Vietnam, Cambodia, Thailand, and Malaysia. Upon his return to Venice, Polo found the city embroiled in war with the rival merchant city of Genoa. Genoese soldiers captured and imprisoned him. While in jail, the stories he told of the people, places, and plants he had seen captured the imagination of all who heard. Polo said of pepper, found on the west coast of India, "You are to understand that the trees that produce pepper are planted and watered—they are not wild."

Polo's stories were written down by a fellow prisoner and titled *The Book of Marco Polo*. Two centuries later, the volume inspired such explorers as Christopher Columbus.

A European map depicts Marco Polo and his relatives on their Asian journey.

The Crusaders sailed to war in galley ships, which sailors rowed when there was insufficient wind.

wide swath of territory that extended from Spain across North Africa and into China. Trade fell off between Europe, which was mostly Christian, and the solidly Islamic Middle East. What few spices straggled into Europe were to be found in palaces and monasteries—isolated places of wealth and learning. Most Europeans had to content themselves with mustard, horseradish, and herbs (many of which were familiar as medicines but were becoming popular as flavorings).

From 1095 to 1300, Europeans embarked on the Crusades, a series of holy wars in Palestine (also called the Holy Land), a Middle Eastern region along the far eastern coast of the Mediterranean Sea. Leaders of the Christian church intended to win the Holy Land from the armies of Islam. The wars created an opportunity for Europeans and Middle Easterners to exchange ideas and goods, as well as to knock heads. The wars revitalized trade between the two groups, and spices became a hot ticket again in Europe.

From the 1400s onward, well-to-do Europeans relied upon Asian spices considerably to make their bland meats and vegetables come to life. They commonly used and mixed their spices in a way that we would consider heavy-handed. Europeans jealously fought over trade in the five "noble spices"—pepper, ginger, cinnamon, clove, and nutmeg. Seafaring nations tried to undercut each other by finding alternate routes to (and sources of) spices.

Spice Wars

In 1492 Christopher Columbus, an Italian sailing on behalf of Spain, set out for spice country in "the Indies" (Southeast Asia) to the east by sailing west. We all know what he found instead. The first European to encounter the American tropics, which he called the West Indies, Columbus paved the way for American spices to enter Europe and for various European powers to claim territory on the newly revealed continents.

In 1498 the Portuguese explorer Vasco da Gama became the first European to find an all-sea route to India. For the next 451 years, Portugal would control the Indian spice trade from the port city of Goa, India. The Portuguese moved on to capture strategic positions in present-day Sri Lanka and Malaysia as well. In 1511 the Portuguese became the first Europeans to reach the Molucca Islands—also called the Spice

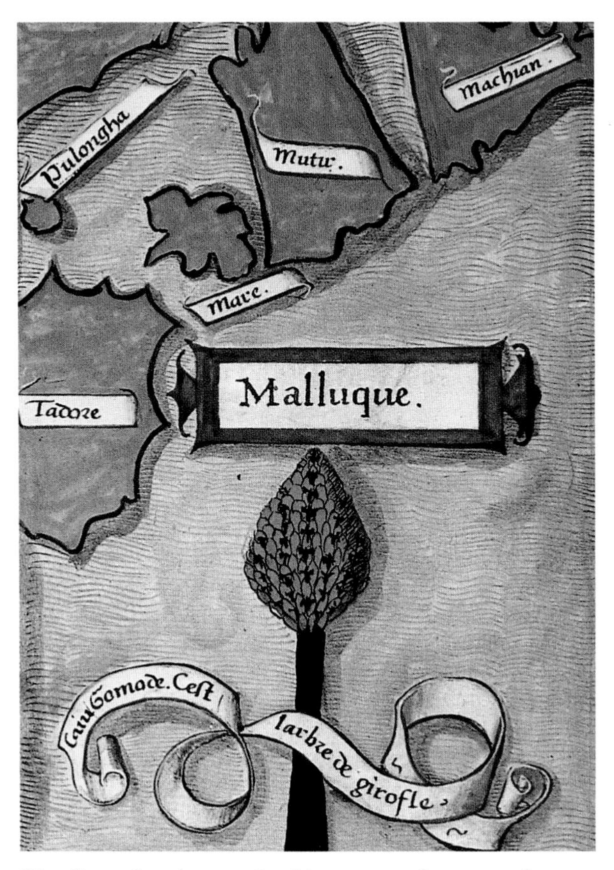

The French, who made this map, and many other European explorers focused on the Moluccas.

Islands—of modern-day Indonesia, the original home of many important seasonings. For years the Portuguese thwarted their English, Spanish, and Dutch seagoing rivals by distributing false maps of the region, designed to lure ships away from the islands and into dangerous waters. The Portuguese ruled the Moluccan spice trade until Spain took control of the islands in 1580.

In 1600 the British formed the British East India Company and wrestled control of India from the Portuguese. Two years later, the Dutch established the Dutch East India Company to handle their spice trade. Soon they dominated Indonesia. The Dutch stopped at nothing in their pursuit of profit. They destroyed plantations to reduce supply and raise prices. They decimated the human populations of islands when local rulers got in the way of business.

The Dutch tightly controlled their Moluccan spice plantations. Even so, in the mid-1700s, a French spy named Pierre Poivre (his name translates to English as Peter Pepper) managed to smuggle several key spice plants out of Indonesia. France and other countries began plantations of their own in the tropical Americas and in Africa. With larger supplies and more merchants competing for sales, spices became available at more reasonable prices.

The power and wealth of the spice trade was limited largely to European colonial powers and built on the labor of the original inhabitants of spice-growing countries. They planted, nurtured, and harvested the spices that made their foreign occupiers rich. Well

Pierre Poivre

Pierre Poivre was born in 1719 in the prosperous river-port town of Lyons, France. As a young man, he studied for the priesthood. A visit to Asia in 1740 sparked Poivre's interest in commerce, however, and his next seven years were spent establishing businesses in the lands that would one day become Vietnam. Next Poivre went to the Moluccas, where he began a glorious career of smuggling fruit and spice trees to the French-held islands of Mauritius and Réunion (both in the Indian Ocean off Madagascar). His efforts were a deliberate attempt to undo Dutch domination of the spice trade and bring exotic flavorings to a wider market at a better price.

into the twentieth century, native peoples in many parts of Asia were under the thumb of European colonists getting rich on their adopted countries' spices.

Modern Days

These days major multinational corporations, not seafaring adventurers, compete for market share in the spice trade. Countries such as India, Indonesia, Tanzania, Madagascar, and Sri Lanka control their own spice industries. Many spices grow outside their regions of origin. Transportation, communication, and marketing have turned the spice story from a saga of mystery, greed, and conquest to a tale of excellent access to the world's resources. In most supermarkets, shoppers can find the tropical spices right next to the herbs, seeds, and roots that have been growing in temperate backyards all along.

In *Flavor Foods: Spices & Herbs,* these celebrated foods are classified according to the plant parts from which they come. We'll begin at the top with spices made from flowers—cloves, capers, and saffron—and work our way to fruits such as pepper and vanilla. There'll be time to check out basil, rosemary, mint, and parsley—all leafy herbs—and cinnamon, the bark of a tree. We'll examine roots and rhizomes—horseradish, licorice, ginger, and turmeric. Finally, we'll look at seeds such as mustard, dill, cumin, and caraway, plus the seed nutmeg and its seed coat, mace.

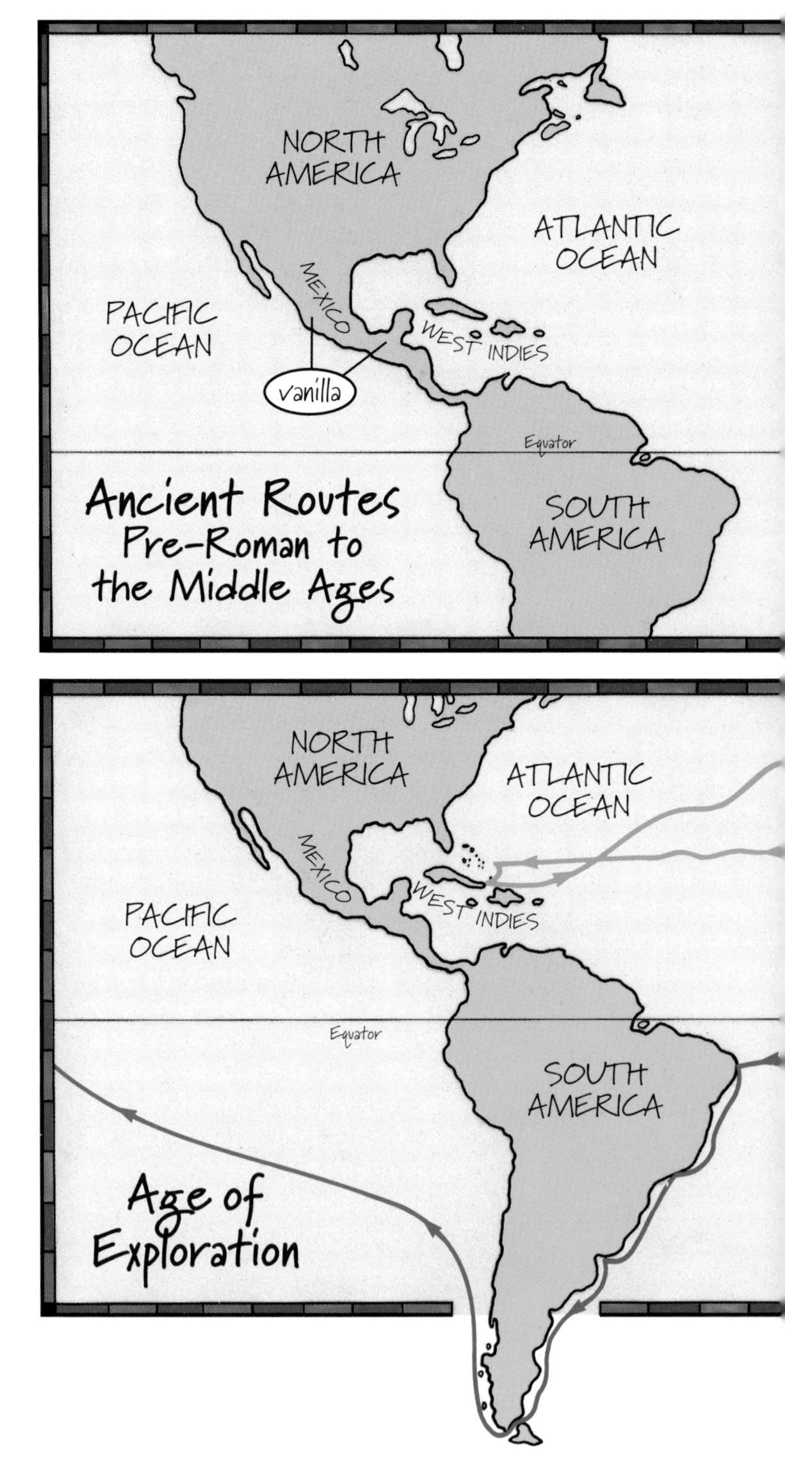

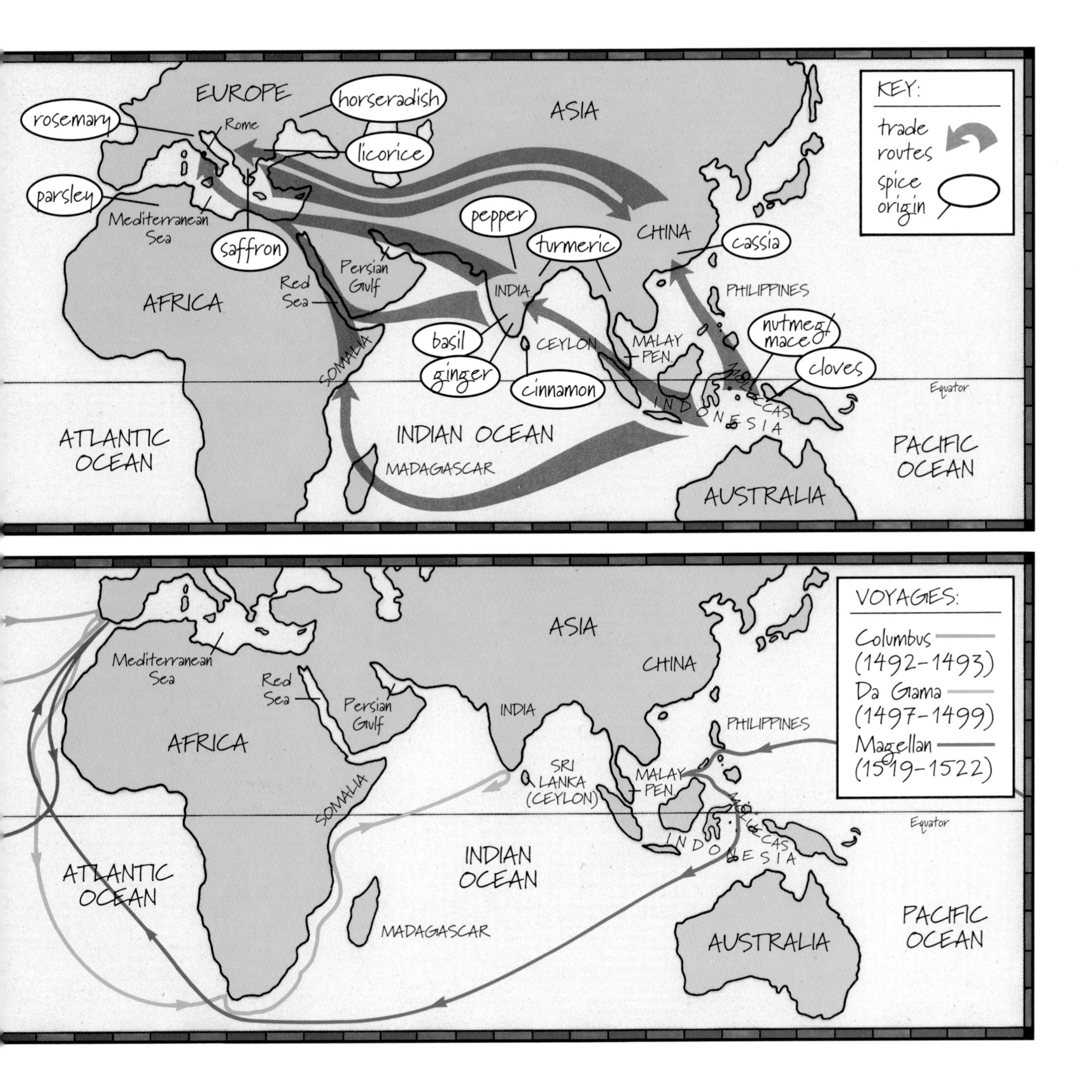
EUROPE
ASIA
KEY:
trade routes
spice origin
rosemary
Rome
horseradish
licorice
parsley
Mediterranean Sea
saffron
pepper
turmeric
CHINA
cassia
Persian Gulf
Red Sea
AFRICA
INDIA
PHILIPPINES
basil
CEYLON
MALAY PEN.
nutmeg/mace
ginger
cinnamon
cloves
SOMALIA
MOLUCCAS
INDONESIA
Equator
ATLANTIC OCEAN
INDIAN OCEAN
MADAGASCAR
AUSTRALIA
PACIFIC OCEAN
VOYAGES:
Columbus (1492–1493)
Da Gama (1497–1499)
Magellan (1519–1522)
ASIA
CHINA
Mediterranean Sea
Red Sea
Persian Gulf
INDIA
PHILIPPINES
AFRICA
SRI LANKA (CEYLON)
MALAY PEN.
SOMALIA
MOLUCCAS
Equator
INDONESIA
INDIAN OCEAN
ATLANTIC OCEAN
MADAGASCAR
AUSTRALIA
PACIFIC OCEAN

Flowers

[*Eugenia caryophyllus*—clove]
[*Crocus sativus*—saffron]

Usually colorful and often scented, the flower is the gateway to the plant's reproductive parts. Most flowers contain stamens—the pollen-producing male organs—and pistils—the female organs that hold the plant's egg cells. The pistil is made up of three parts: the stigma, style, and ovary. Many flowers also have showy, fragrant petals. Petals attract the insects or birds on which the plant relies to achieve pollination—the uniting of **pollen** grains with egg cells. If pollination occurs, the flower will develop into a fruit that holds the plant's seeds.

Imagine anyone deciding to eat the dried flower buds of a tree. That's what cloves are. The 40-foot-tall tropical tree on which they grow is native to Indonesia. As the tree's leaves mature, they change from yellow to pink to shiny green. The flower buds also change color and must be picked just as they turn light pink.

The word *clove* comes from *clavo* or *clou*, Spanish and French words meaning "nail." The dried buds resemble small, dark tacks.

Nose, nose, nose, nose!
And who gave you
that jolly red nose?
Cinnamon and ginger,
nutmegs and cloves,
And that gave me
my jolly red nose.

—Thomas Ravenscroft

Saffron makes the cake
yellow....

—German folk song

In the Molucca Islands and in neighboring India, people had been cooking with cloves since time immemorial when the ancient Chinese began purchasing the spice from Indians, perhaps around 100 B.C. At that time, members of the Chinese court customarily sweetened their breath with cloves before presenting themselves to the emperor.

By the A.D. 300s—and possibly long before—Arab trading ships were bringing cloves from the Moluccas to Mediterranean ports in modern-day Lebanon and Syria. In 335 Constantine, ruler of the Roman Empire, received a delivery of cloves at his capital city of Constantinople (modern Istanbul, Turkey). He promptly sent more than 80 pounds of the spice, packed in jars, to the pope (leader of the Christian

Family Matters

To keep things straight in the huge families of plants and animals, scientists classify and name living things by grouping them according to shared features within each of seven major categories. The categories are kingdom, division or phylum, class, order, family, genus, and species. Species share the most features in common, while members of a kingdom or division share far fewer traits. This system of scientific classification and naming is called taxonomy. Scientists refer to plants and animals by a two-part Latin or Greek term made up of the genus and the species name. The genus name comes first, followed by the species name. When talking about a genus that has more than one commonly cultivated species, such as *Brassica* (mustard), we'll use only the genus name in the chapter heading. In the discussions about specific spice plants, we'll list the two-part species name. Look at the clove's taxonomic name on page 18. Can you figure out to what genus the clove belongs? And to what species?

German merchants were among the few medieval Europeans with money to buy cloves.

church) in Rome, demonstrating simultaneously his generosity and his power. Cloves were among the world's most expensive spices and so made an impressive gift.

Costly cloves were most likely not the condiment of the masses. But in the 800s, monastery scribes reported Swiss monks sprinkling the spice on their fish. By 973 German merchants were seasoning their meals with it. Rulers of the Asian islands where the buds grew became rich on the clove trade. Powerful people in Europe began to take note.

A Portuguese ship captain named Francisco Serrão arrived in the Moluccas in 1511. He settled on one of the clove islands, never to budge again. He sent word about the clove bounty to a family member, Ferdinand Magellan, who was a navigator for the king of Spain. While searching for an alternate route to the Moluccas, Magellan's fleet completed the first voyage around the globe. (Alas, Magellan himself died on the trip.) But the expedition failed to make new inroads into the clove business. As the sole importers, the Portuguese made a fortune and became the clove emperors of Europe. Establishing military bases in the Spice Islands and making treaties with Moluccan leaders, the Portuguese began shipping cloves exclusively to their capital city of Lisbon, then sending the spice on to other European capitals.

Go ahead, make a pomander! A what? A pomander is a scented creation made from a mix of aromatic substances. It's a lovely small gift for anyone, anytime. It's also a common, old-fashioned Christmas decoration.

You will need an orange and a large handful of whole cloves. Stick the cloves artfully into the orange, covering as much of the fruit's surface as you can. If you feel clever, make a colorful bow out of ribbon and attach it to the top of the orange with a straight pin. Display your handiwork on the dining room table or another dry place for a while until the orange has shriveled up a bit.

Then liven up your sock drawer, your closet, or another dull-smelling place with your fragrant trinket.

The Portuguese soon made cloves more readily available to the middle-class European purchaser. By the close of the 1500s, though, the Dutch had taken over Portuguese holdings in the Spice Islands, murdered rival English clove growers and thousands of Moluccans, and cut down countless clove trees to preserve just enough for their own trade. Their single-minded obsession was to limit any and all competition.

Ultimately Dutch tactics brought about the Dutch traders' own downfall. Due to the elimination of too many trees, the clove industry virtually ceased in the Moluccas.

Meanwhile, spice saboteur Pierre Poivre planted stolen clove trees on the islands of Réunion and Mauritius in the late 1700s. Poivre's political enemies in France felt that these trees succeeded all too well and brought Poivre too much power. So they arranged to destroy all but one of Poivre's clove trees. That one is said to be the ancestor of all modern-day clove trees.

In the late 1700s, clove trees from Mauritius traveled to the islands of Zanzibar and Pemba, parts of the modern-day East African country of Tanzania. Sultan Said of Zanzibar, who ruled from 1804 to 1856, planted clove seedlings in his gardens. When he saw how they thrived, he insisted that the local estate owners plant three clove trees for every coconut palm. If the planters resisted, the sultan suggested, they would lose their holdings. Because they obeyed, the resulting clove industry brought prosperity to Zanzibar for years to come. In the port at Zanzibar Town, colossal pyramids of the dark, dried buds scented the air near the docks. Sultan Said's influence led the region to become the world's leading source of cloves. These days up to 75 percent of the country's total exports derive from the clove business, most of which is centered on Pemba.

Growing Cloves

Thanks to Sultan Said, Tanzania is one of the world's biggest clove-exporting countries.

A clove tree grows on an Indonesian plantation.

Madagascar is another high producer. Sri Lanka, Indonesia, Malaysia, and Grenada also farm fragrant cloves.

Growers plant their trees from seed, often in shaded areas. Clove trees must grow for at least five years before they begin to flower. Many trees live to be 100 years old or more.

Clove buds require hand picking at just the right moment, before they burst into flower. Each tree must be picked over several times to insure every bud is caught. A typical tree can produce no more than about 10 pounds of the tiny flower buds. Often women and children pick the lower branches, and men on bamboo ladders pick the higher branches. In Zanzibar the harvest employs as many as 40,000 workers. Because of the high cost of all the hand labor, cloves are relatively expensive.

Workers sort and clean the harvested cloves. Next the buds dry in the sun for two days. Then they are ready for the removal of their outer coat. Workers supervise another several days of drying before the cloves are ready for market. The buds change color from green to brown during the drying process.

Clove Oil Goes High Tech

Clove stems are a source of a valuable oil that contains a chemical substance called eugenol. Eugenol has many uses. It's a painkiller for toothaches and is also found in mouthwashes and perfumes. (In fact, the finest perfumes in the world are made in part from oil extracted from the clove buds themselves.) Eugenol aids in making artificial vanillin. Meat packers treat their products with eugenol, a natural bacteria fighter, to prevent spoiling. Finally, scientists use eugenol to prepare slides for viewing with a microscope.

Eating Cloves

In the United States, people stud baked hams with whole cloves. Ground cloves are part of a famous Indian spice mix called *garam masala.* The spice also flavors cakes, breads, pickles, and sauces in Europe and North America. A little dash of ground cloves will bring out the flavor of beef in a stew or gravy.

Many U.S. Christian families celebrate Christmas or Easter with a clove-laced ham.

Laborers hand harvest the stigmas from each saffron crocus *(inset)*.

Saffron

The stigma of a crocus flower ~~that blooms~~ only for two weeks, saffron is the rarest (and most expensive) of the spices. Each purple flower contains only three of the tiny, reddish-yellow strands. A pound of saffron consists of 200,000 stigmas. Imagine the acres of flowers necessary to secure even a modest pinch of this spice! To be fair, one needs only a tiny amount of saffron to sense its presence—about a quarter teaspoon at most for many dishes.

Saffron is a labor-intensive crop, and therefore it was most popular when people of uncommon wealth had access to workers who toiled without pay—that is, slaves. Slave-keeping people such as the Moguls (who ruled India in the 1500s and 1600s) and the Ottoman Turks (whose far-flung empire started in the 1300s and peaked in the 1500s and 1600s) loved saffron.

Probably native to Greece, *Crocus sativus* was familiar to ancient peoples of the eastern Mediterranean, such as the Romans and the Egyptians. Saffron was a popular ingredient in foods. It made a bright-yellow dye and a perfume. The Romans happily scattered the precious spice across roadways to make carpets on which the glorious feet of their rulers could tread. Minoan artists of ancient Crete, an island off the Greek mainland, depicted the saffron harvest on the walls of the palace of Knossos, which was probably built before 100 B.C.

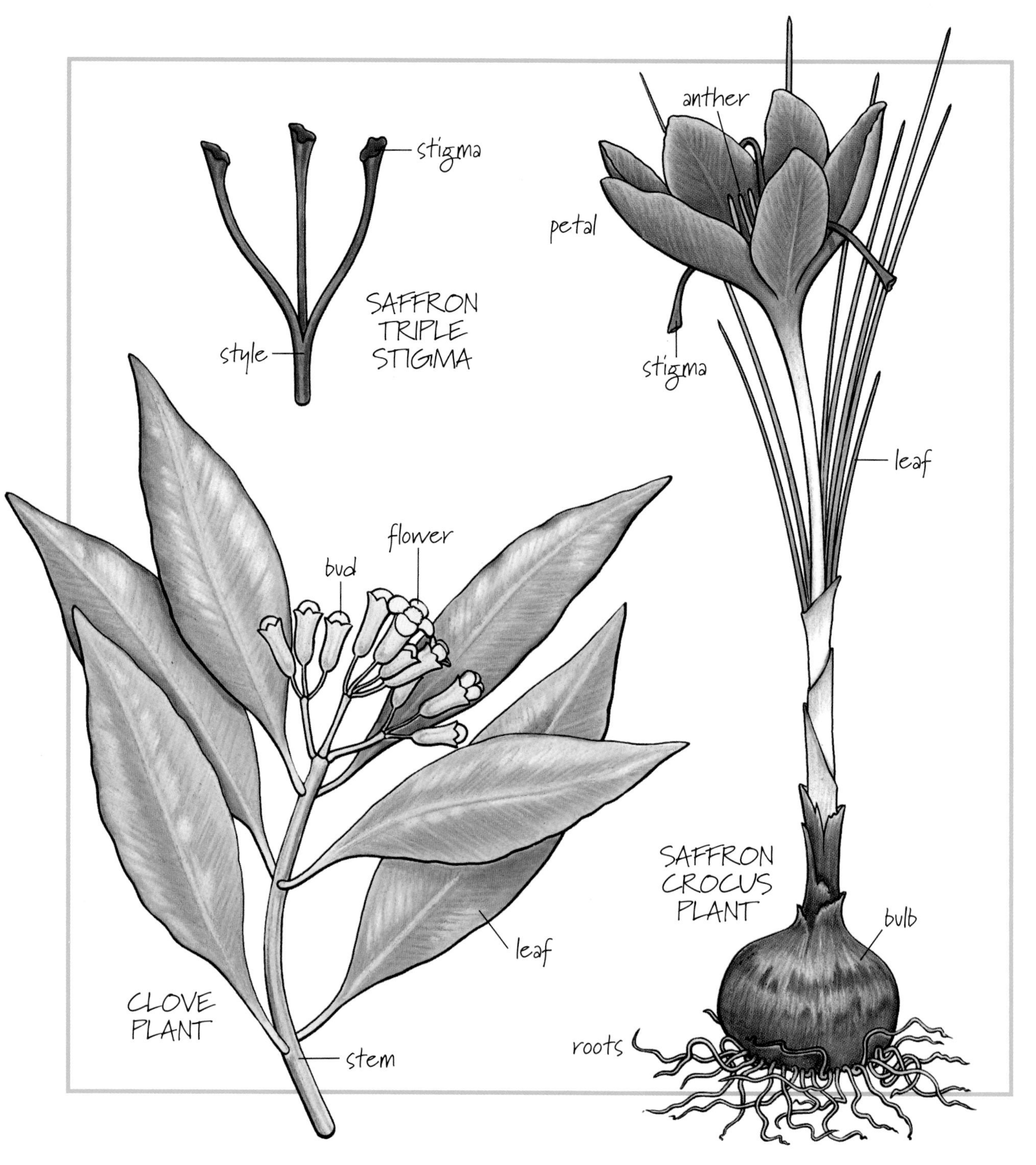
stigma
SAFFRON
TRIPLE
STIGMA
style
anther
petal
stigma
leaf
flower
bud
leaf
CLOVE
PLANT
stem
SAFFRON
CROCUS
PLANT
bulb
roots

By the A.D. 600s, saffron had reached China, probably via Arab traders. The Moors (Arabs from North Africa) likely brought the saffron crocus to Spain in the 700s. Four centuries later, contact between European and Arab merchants during the Crusades renewed the European demand for saffron. The spice appeared in Germany and France in the 1100s and then in England a few hundred years later.

A town in southern England still carries the name Saffron Walden, though its saffron-growing days are long gone. During the Middle Ages (roughly from A.D. 500 to 1500), the area around Walden, as the central market town was then called, was a major sheep-raising and cloth-making area. An unknown entrepreneur smuggled saffron crocuses from Spain into Walden and planted them as a source of dye for wool cloth. But English weather didn't suit the plant well, and it was not a dependable crop. Saffron production died out there by the early 1700s.

Saffron became quite common among an uncommon group of Americans—the Amish. In the 1700s, one Amish family emigrated from their native Germany to Pennsylvania. They brought crocuses—the basis of the saffron business that had been their calling back home. The crocuses flourished in Pennsylvania, and ever since, saffron has been a common spice in Amish noodle dishes, soups, and special baked goods.

Growing Saffron

These days saffron is grown commercially in Iran, India, Spain, France, Greece, Turkey, and Morocco. But wherever people grow saffron, they tend it carefully. In middle to late summer, farmers plant the

Cut a Caper

The caper is another unopened bud valued for its flavor. It grows on a spiky, trailing shrub—*Caparis spinoza*—native to Saharan Africa or perhaps the Mediterranean. Capers are always pickled whole in a vinegary brine. A common ingredient in Mediterranean cuisines, they turn up most frequently in sauces and salads. You may have eaten them on pizza.

crocus bulb in sunny fields of well-drained, sandy soil. The plant grows to a height of about six inches. The flowers appear in the fall. In the early hours of the morning, pickers gather the flowers by hand and place them in baskets. Workers must then sort through the flowers and remove the three stigmas, called threads, from each blossom. In one technique, the person holds the crocus in the left hand and uses one finger to remove the flower's style. He or she then pinches out the stigmas with the fingers of the right hand.

Spanish saffron growers dry the harvested stigmas over coal fires. They check the saffron for cleanliness, then pack it in small paper envelopes or slender glass tubes. The world's most labor-intensive spice is then ready to be shipped to market.

Eating Saffron

Spaniards use saffron liberally in the national rice dish, paella. Saffron is popular in other parts of the Mediterranean as well—the French put it in bouillabaisse, a fish soup, and Italians like it in a rice dish called risotto. In more northerly parts of Europe, such as Germany and Britain, saffron colors baked goods such as cakes and breads. Greeks, Turks, and Indians add saffron to rice, soups, and stews. The spice figures frequently in Asian folk remedies for headaches, digestive troubles, and even as an antidepressant. It is also used in perfumes, as a cosmetic, and as a food coloring.

A Spanish cook serves up a plateful of his paella.

Paella
(6 servings)

12 small fresh clams in shells (optional)
12 medium fresh shrimp in shells (optional)
8 ounces chorizo or garlicky sausage
2 tablespoons olive oil
1 2½-pound chicken, cut into 8 pieces
4 cups chicken broth
1 medium-sized onion, cut into wedges
1 sweet red or green pepper, cleaned out and cut into strips
½ teaspoon minced garlic
2 cups white rice, uncooked
½ teaspoon oregano
¼ teaspoon saffron
½ cup fresh or frozen peas

Every town and village in Spain has its own version of paella. Rice is the only absolutely vital ingredient, but almost all Spaniards agree that the dish needs saffron, too.

Cover the clams in salty water (3 tablespoons salt to 8 cups water), soak 15 minutes, and rinse. Repeat twice. Remove the shrimp shells and split them down the back with a small knife. Remove the large vein. Rinse and dry the shrimp.

In a paella pan or large, ovenproof skillet, cook the sausage. Remove it from the pan, cool, and slice. Heat the olive oil in the skillet and brown the chicken 15 minutes, turning occasionally. Remove and set it aside. In a saucepan, heat the chicken broth to a boil. Meanwhile, brown the onion, pepper, and garlic in the skillet. Remove the racks from your oven and preheat to 400°. Add the rice, boiling broth, oregano, and saffron to the skillet. Bring the food to a boil over high heat and then remove the pan from the heat. Arrange the meat and seafood on top of the rice. Scatter the peas over all. Set the pan on the oven floor and bake uncovered until the liquid is absorbed, about 25 minutes. Never stir the paella after it goes into the oven!

Remove the paella from the oven and cover it with a kitchen towel. Let it rest 5 minutes, then serve at the table directly from the pan.

Fruits

[*Piper nigrum*—pepper]
[*Vanilla planifolia*—vanilla]

When flowers are pollinated, fruit is the result. Fruits are the developed ovaries of flowers and contain the plant's seeds. The bright berries of the viny pepper plant and the long pods of the vanilla orchid are the fruits of plants.

Pepper

Black pepper, the most common spice in the world, comes from a dark green, climbing vine. It produces spikes of white flowers that develop into small, green berries. The fruits turn red as they ripen. Pepper originated in India at least 4,000 years ago. The pepper plant's name in Sanskrit, the ancient language of India, was *pippeli*. In Latin the name became *piper*, from which the English word *pepper* derives.

Black, white, green, and pink peppercorns. The colorful berries sold as pink peppercorns aren't really peppercorns at all. They're the fruit of the pepper tree, *Schinus molle*, an evergreen from Peru that is not related to *Piper nigrum*.

Don't be too daring in the kitchen. . . . Stay with safe things, like pepper.

—Bruce Jay Friedman

Ah, you flavour everything; you are the vanilla of society.

—Sydney Smith

Pepper vines cover trees in an Indian forest *(left)*. Sales of the plant's berries *(above)* make up one-fourth of the world's spice trade.

While the first pepper harvesters probably worked from wild vines, historians think pepper was cultivated early in India. Growers trained pepper vines on wooden **trellises** or on rows of trees planted specifically for that purpose.

Small batches of pepper trickled into the Mediterranean part of the world, brought by Arabs who probably bought the spice from other traders. Pepper was the first pungent spice to arrive in Europe. By the 400s B.C., the people of early Rome were keen to have pepper, both for use as a medicine and as a flavoring in food. The Roman emperor Domitian built a spice market in the Roman Forum around A.D. 80 or 90 and named the primary road leading into the market Via Piperatica, or Pepper Way.

At the height of the Roman Empire, expensive pepper had snob appeal as well as culinary use. If you possessed far more pepper than you could use, you were an important person indeed. Foreign dignitaries arriving in Rome ceremoniously handed out parcels of pepper to senators and generals, whose own spice cupboards were already filled with the precious berry.

Although pepper was widely used—the Romans even sprinkled it on their desserts—for hundreds of years, people didn't know where the spice came from. The Arabs kept their sources secret to maintain a monopoly on the supply. The Roman emperor Augustus, who ruled from 27 B.C. to A.D. 14, sent a group of soldiers into Arabia to find the route to the valued spice. The Arabs they consulted for directions deliberately misled them, so the overland route they took turned out to be a wild goose chase.

Pliny the Elder, a Roman naturalist, wondered that the ordinary-looking pepper vine and its fruit were ever noticed at all. "Who was the first person to try this on his meat?" he wrote.

By A.D. 408, Rome, under attack by invaders from the north, was desperately offering pepper to its enemies. That year Alaric, leader of the invading Visigoths, demanded and received 3,000 pounds of pepper from the Romans. Within the century, Rome ran out of luck, and the mighty empire broke apart. For 500 years afterward, the commercial vigor of the region slowed, the spice trade to Europe was curtailed, and pepper was once again hard to come by.

A Roman soldier and a northern European warrior face off in this Roman stone carving.

This European painting from the 1300s depicts Indians harvesting pepper.

From the fall of Rome onward, merchants from Venice sailed to the spice markets of Alexandria. There they could do business with Arab traders who brought Asian spices to Egypt via overland routes. At the start of the Crusades in 1095, Venetian sailors began transporting fighting forces from Europe to the Holy Land. On the return voyage, the merchants packed their empty ships with Indian pepper.

Throughout the Middle Ages, gold and silver were coined by all manner of people, and the coins' value was inconsistent. Peppercorns were a more reliable means of exchange. A pound of peppercorns could pay a laborer in England for two weeks' work. Peppercorns could pay the rent, pay a ransom, secure a bride, or serve as a bribe.

Pick Your Pepper

For generations people have confused pepper, the pungent black powder, and pepper, the pungent red or green vegetable. The confusion stems from the 1492 voyage of Christopher Columbus, who was determined to bring black pepper, *Piper nigrum*, to Spain from India. Landing in the Americas, Columbus latched onto the first spicy thing he could find and named it "pepper." That fateful food was *Capsicum frutescans*, the chili pepper—unrelated to black pepper. Europeans soon began to grow chili peppers, which are incidentally another fruit spice. In certain places, the red powder made from dried chilies pushed expensive, Asian-grown black pepper aside.

In the late 1500s, Chinese traders sold pepper to the Portuguese from the port of Macao in southeastern China.

The search for pepper was one reason that Europeans began to explore the globe in the 1400s. Throughout the 1500s and 1600s, Europeans continued to seek pepper. In the process they established colonies and businesses all over the world. After a time, many of these colonies—including the United States of America—broke ties with their mother countries to continue doing business on their own.

In the new United States, pepper remained a moneymaker. Salem, Massachusetts, a New England seaport, was once known as the Pepper Port. For almost a century, beginning in 1797, the ships of Salem brought pepper from Southeast Asia. The first ship captain to make the trip earned seven times the amount of money he'd spent on the voyage. In 1805 about 7.5 million pounds of pepper passed through Salem on its way to U.S. buyers.

Pirates ended the American pepper bonanza. For years the U.S. Navy escorted the clipper ships, protecting their spicy cargoes from European and American buccaneers looking for easy prey. The U.S. government eventually decided it could no longer afford to pay for such far-flung naval exploits, and heavy U.S. involvement in the pepper trade ended.

Up and Up with Pepper Growing

The tropical pepper plant relishes long periods of rain and high temperatures. It thrives best with some shade. In the wild, the plant climbs tall trees with leaves that provide cover. In India pepper growers follow nature. They let their vines climb trees that soar as high as 40 or 50 feet.

Farmers make stem cuttings of the vine and plant them in rich, well-worked soil at the base of trees or wooden supports set about three feet apart. Growers wait about three years for their first harvest, but thereafter they can harvest annually for 10 to 15 years. Harvest in India takes place in June and July. Workers climb tall ladders and snap off stems that hold from 5 to 30 green berries each.

A Malaysian laborer spreads green pepper berries on mats to dry.

In Brazil and Sumatra, Indonesia, where large tracts of land are available, pepper vines are allowed to grow only 5 or 6 feet high on stakes.

Peppercorns from the same plant produce different types of pepper. Green or fresh pepper is the unripe fruit picked young and often eaten whole, rather than dried and ground. Black pepper, as well, comes from unripe peppercorns. People sun-dry the fruit on rooftops or in flat, open areas for a few days, during which time the green berries turn black. At this point, they are ready for shipping whole or grinding into powder. For white pepper, the berries are allowed to ripen fully. Workers pick the fruits and soak them in water so that the outer husk comes off easily. Then the white pepper is dried.

Each year Indonesia and Brazil grow a combined 50 percent of the world's 220,000 tons of pepper. Southern India provides another 40 percent. In the state of Kerala, India, the port city of Cochin is the shipping point for pepper. Local buyers acquire pepper from area farmers and then sell the goods to exporters, who send trucks to collect the harvest. At the port, workers clean the pepper before shipping it abroad. Different markets of the world require differing levels of cleanliness. In the United States, large spice companies clean the pepper again before processing.

Allspice

Allspice, *Pimenta dioica*, is the berry of a tree native to the West Indies and Central America. Close relative to the clove, allspice refuses to thrive anywhere but in its homeland. The best berries come from Jamaica. Allspice earned its name because it tastes like a mix of pepper, cloves, cinnamon, and nutmeg or mace.

Nothing to Sneeze At

The United States is the world's largest importer of pepper, buying close to 42,500 tons a year. India and Indonesia each provide one-third of U.S. imports, and Brazil supplies about one-quarter. Malaysia, Thailand, Sri Lanka, Mexico, Vietnam, and China also sell pepper to the United States. The world pepper market is worth about $500 million dollars annually.

As with many agricultural items, pepper production and subsequent pricing is often affected by various factors. In the 1990s, dry weather in India reduced pepper harvests. At the same time, years of low prices for Indonesian pepper led some plantation owners to neglect their vines, possibly turning away from pepper to more profitable crops. The resulting shortage on the world market caused prices to rise rapidly.

Indian workers pack black pepper for shipment to market.

A spice seller in Bombay, India, offers peppercorns among his wares.

Receipt for Your Peppercorn?

On Peppercorn Day, April 23, officials of the Bermuda government collect the annual rent of one peppercorn from other officials for the use of the Old State House in St. George, which was the country's capital during its days as a British colony. The custom dates back to the Middle Ages and derives from the British tradition of peppercorn rents.

The Pleasures of Pepper

All over the world, people pop peppercorns into stews, soups, pickles, and marinades. Diners sprinkle pepper on everything. The best is fresh pepper, ground in a heavy pepper mill right when you want it. Some say the next best use of pepper is on steak. For the French dish *steak au poivre,* cooks press thick tenderloins of beef into a bed of crushed black peppercorns. Then they grill the meat and serve it with a peppery white sauce. French and Belgian cooks often mix green peppercorns with cream and lemon juice for a pepper sauce good on both meat and fish. Practically all processed meats, from hot dogs to lunchmeats, contain pepper. It appears in baked goods, spice mixes, sauces, and all manner of canned and frozen foods. For centuries black pepper was a key ingredient in Indian curries, although the unrelated chili pepper has largely replaced it.

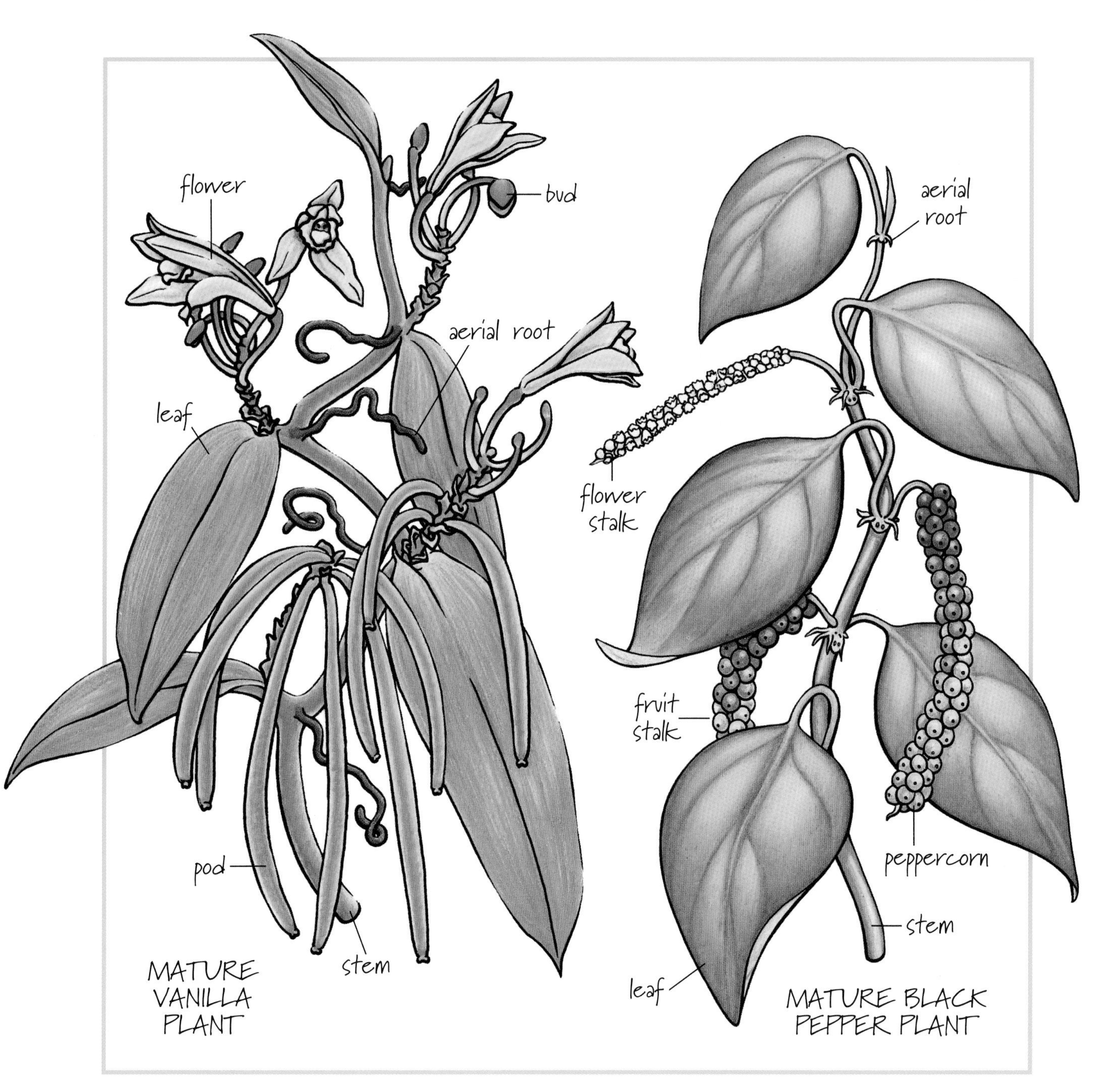
flower
bud
aerial root
leaf
pod
stem
MATURE VANILLA PLANT
aerial root
flower stalk
fruit stalk
peppercorn
stem
leaf
MATURE BLACK PEPPER PLANT

Green vanilla pods are ready to pick.

Vanilla

Vanilla is the only member of the extensive family of orchids—the largest plant family in the world—that people use as food. Native to Mexico and Central America, vanilla is a viny plant that seeks out a host to climb and may measure as long as 350 feet. Vanilla vines produce yellow-white flowers that turn into long, slender, green pods. The vanilla pod is called a bean, but it contains the tiniest of seeds, which have nothing beanlike about them.

The Totonacs grew vanilla in forest plantations.

The Totonacs, who in ancient times lived in what would become the state of Veracruz, Mexico, prized vanilla not only as a flavoring but as an insect-repelling perfume. In 1425 the Aztecs, who dominated present-day Mexico from the 1300s until the 1520s, conquered the Totonacs and demanded a portion of their vanilla harvests.

The Aztecs first mixed vanilla and chocolate, a combination that is still popular throughout the world. They paired the two flavors in a beverage called *chocolatl,* sometimes sweetened with honey, sometimes unsweetened, and occasionally enlivened with hot chili peppers. The Aztecs called vanilla *tlilxochitl* (tleel-shoh-CHEE-tl). Spaniards—who colonized Mexico in the 1500s—found the word too tough for their tongues and renamed the plant *vainilla,* meaning "little pod." The Spaniards soon brought the pod home to Europe.

A vanilla flower bursts into bloom.

The Food of the Gods

Chocolate and cocoa both come from the cacao tree, a native of Central America. The pods of the 15- to 30-foot tree grow directly on the trunk and main branches. The seeds inside these pods are called cacao beans. Maya and Aztec Indians were processing cultivated cacao beans as early as A.D. 600. They considered chocolate a sacred food. From this notion, the tree takes its taxonomic name, *Theobroma cacao,* which means "cacao, food of the gods."

Vanilla across the Ocean

Queen Elizabeth I of England first sampled vanilla in 1602 when her personal pharmacist offered some. He also passed some pods to his peers in Europe and so spread interest in the plant. Well before people ate vanilla with any frequency, vanilla orchids were growing in the French royal greenhouses near Paris.

By the 1700s, French colonials in Mexico were growing vanilla. By the next century, they had discovered new ways to pollinate the tricky plant. They had also developed vanilla plantings among their extensive sugarcane plantations on various French-held tropical islands, which at the time included Réunion, Tahiti, Mauritius, and Madagascar. Tahitians eventually developed a local species of vanilla orchid.

Vanilla caught the attention of U.S. gardener-statesman (and soon to be president) Thomas Jefferson, who first encountered the pods during travels in France in the 1780s. One day in Philadelphia, Pennsylvania, Jefferson had a vanilla craving and sent his butler to the local market to find some. The man returned empty handed, stating that vanilla beans were unknown in the city. Jefferson

Vanilla Pollination

The first plantings of vanilla orchids in European greenhouses produced glorious flowers and healthy vines, but no pods. They were too far from the tropical American bees (or possibly hummingbirds) that pollinate the orchids in the wild. In the 1840s, a gardener and former slave from Réunion named Edmond Albius perfected the art of hand pollination using a bamboo sliver. His technique allowed the success of large vanilla plantations in tropical lands far from the vine's origins.

Farmers have set brand-new vanilla cuttings on short stakes at this plantation in French Polynesia, an island group in the South Pacific Ocean.

quickly wrote to a colleague in Paris, requesting him to "send me a packet of 50 pods, which may come very well in a packet of newspapers." Vanilla arrived soon thereafter in the young United States.

Growing Vanilla

Commercial vanilla growing requires patience. Growers first plant evergreen trees, spaced about eight feet apart, as supports. After a year, workers plant vanilla vine cuttings at the base of each tree. Three months later, the young vines begin to sprout—and to climb faster than Jack's beanstalk. Farmers cut the vines back to heights that workers can reach. After about five years of growth, vines begin to produce pods. Workers hand pollinate selected flowers—too many flowers clustered together will not produce enough healthy pods.

After about nine months, the vanilla pods are ready for harvest and for the curing process. The fresh-picked pod does not smell like vanilla in the slightest. The laborious curing procedure makes one wonder how people learned to scald, sweat, dry, and condition the slender pods in the first place.

To cure the beans, workers first place the pods in the sun for a dose of heat. Then they wrap the vanilla in layers of fabric and place the bundles in boxes to sweat—that is, to ferment in a warm place. The sweating process turns the pods from green to brown. More heat, either from the sun or from drying devices, comes next. Then the vanilla goes back into boxes for three months of aging.

Finally the pods, at this stage called beans, are sorted, tied together, and placed in cans for shipment around the world. Experts estimate that about 600 pounds of pods produce 120 pounds of cured beans.

The United States, the world's largest customer for vanilla beans, imports almost 47 percent of its vanilla from Indonesia. Madagascar is the next largest source at 39 percent. Ten percent comes from Comoros, an independent island nation off the coast of Madagascar. Mexico, Puerto Rico, and Réunion also export vanilla to the world market. Besides the United States, France and Germany are the world's main importers.

Workers in Réunion sort a batch of vanilla beans, grading them for quality.

Mexican vanilla orchid and cured beans

Divine Vanilla

Ice cream producers use half of the pure vanilla imported to the United States. Vanilla continues to be the most popular ice cream flavor in the United States, comprising one-third of the country's ice cream sales.

Consumers can buy vanilla in two forms—as whole beans or as a liquid extract. Bakers, both at home and in commercial bakeries, use fragrant vanilla to flavor all manner of cakes, confections, cookies, custards, puddings, and pastries. Most chocolate products contain vanilla, and the heady aroma even turns up in perfumes.

VANILLA SUGAR
(2 CUPS)

1 vanilla bean
2 cups white sugar

Looking for something to do with sugar other than sneak it out of the bowl? Try making vanilla sugar. First, go out and buy a vanilla bean—you can usually find them on the spice racks at the supermarket. Place the bean in a jar. Cover it with the sugar. Seal the jar tightly and go about your business. Return in two weeks, open the jar, and sniff. Mmm. Vanilla sugar is the happy result. Make muffins with it, add it to whipped cream, or just, um, sneak a taste, as always.

The same vanilla beans can flavor several batches of sugar.

Leaves

[*Ocimum basilicum*—basil]
[*Rosmarinus officinalis*—rosemary]
[*Petroselinum crispum*—parsley]

The leaf of a plant is its primary organ for making food through photosynthesis. The green leafy plants we call herbs grow everywhere in the world. Each continent and each region has its own native plants that people have used for ages as medicines and in cooking. Some herbs, such as basil (a native of India) and mint (a European herb), are so adaptable that they grow easily almost anywhere.

With the exception of basil, the plants profiled here all originated in Europe and are used worldwide. Many started out in ancient times as medicinal plants. They traveled across Europe with the spread of Roman Catholic monasteries, where for centuries clerics nurtured and protected the plants in walled gardens. Slowly, as people became more familiar with herbs, the leaves crept off the healer's shelf and into the cooking pot.

Basill fine and busht, sow in May.

—Thomas Tusser

Are you going to Scarborough Fair? Parsley, sage, rosemary, and thyme . . . .

—English folk song

For the best flavor, herbs—such as this basil plant—should be picked before their flowers appear.

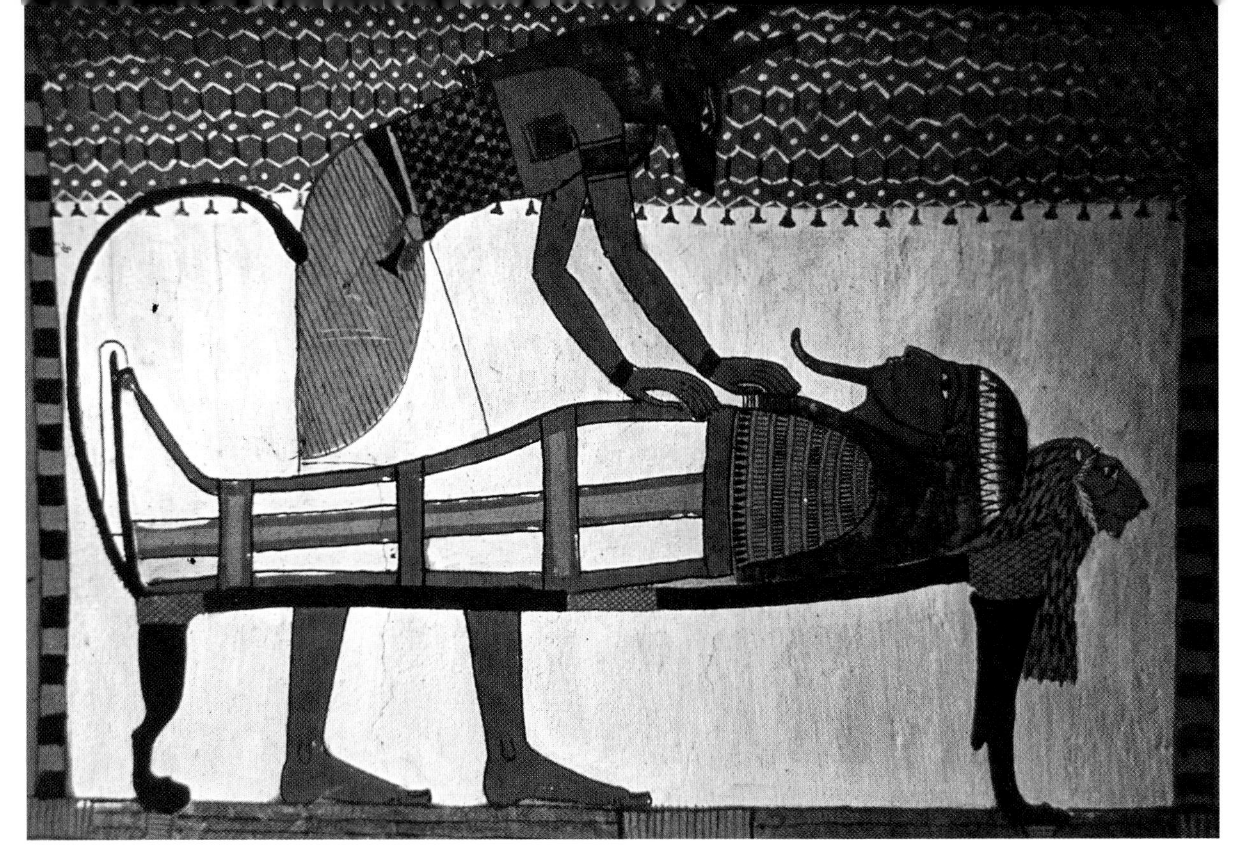

Ancient Egyptians used basil, along with oils, spices, and resins, to make mummies of their dead. Embalming was believed to preserve the bodies for eternal life.

Basil

A sweet-smelling, flavorful plant native to India, basil is grown in many parts of the world as both an herb and an **ornamental,** simply to add fragrance and color to the garden. Some varieties of basil taste like cinnamon, lemon, or even licorice. And the plant comes in at least three colors—deep purple, red, and grass green.

Ancient Indians held the plant as sacred and offered it to the Hindu god Vishnu. The early Egyptians gave basil to their gods and used it with other herbs to prepare mummies. Carried to the Mediterranean at an unknown time by unknown people, basil quickly became a prized culinary and medicinal herb—although reports are mixed as to what health-giving attributes the plant actually had. Some people claimed basil could cure warts, the common cold, or depression. Other people, however, felt that basil attracted scorpions. The ancient Greeks named the plant *basilikon,* meaning "kingly." Stories from more than one culture relate that only a king with a golden sickle could cut the world's first basil. Both the Greeks and the Romans used the herb in sauces, and the Romans favored basil as a symbol of love.

Eating Basil

Pesto—a purée of basil, garlic, Parmesan cheese, pine nuts, and olive oil—comes from the Italian region of Liguria. But you don't have to be Ligurian to love pesto on pasta. Pesto's cousin from southern France is *pistou,* meaning "pounded," a basil-and-garlic mix added to vegetable-bean soup.

Tomatoes and basil are a favorite southern European combination. Basil, fresh tomatoes, mozzarella, and olive oil on crusty bread make a typical Mediterranean open-faced sandwich. Tomato sauces served on Italian pasta usually include basil. In the United States, canned tomatoes are often packed with basil leaves.

At least three tropically grown basil varieties are key to Thai cooking—Thai sweet basil, holy basil, and lemon basil. All three are used in a wide range of stir-fry dishes, and lemon-basil seeds go into ice cream and other dessert treats.

Rosemary

Rosemary is a Mediterranean native that thrives close to the sea, gaining its moisture from the air, but needing little rain. Perhaps for this reason, the Romans gave it the Latin name *ros marinus,* or "dew of the sea." Uniquely, in its genus of plants, it is the only species. Rosemary is a perennial growing on a sturdy, woody base that can reach seven feet in height. Its leaves are small, stiff, and fragrant, its flowers a faint blue.

Ancient Egyptians left sprigs of dried rosemary in their tombs, but we don't know exactly why. They may have found the incenselike aroma of the plant appropriate for a funeral. The plant has long been associated with memory, especially with remembering people.

It's a Fact!

Home gardeners often grow basil between their tomato plants. The two foods taste good together. And basil repels white flies, attracts butterflies and other beneficial insects, and stimulates tomato growth.

Students in ancient Greece wore rosemary wreaths during exams to urge their memories on. And as a memorial gesture, the Romans placed bunches of rosemary in the hands of their dead. Roman women also carried the plant at festive occasions such as weddings.

By the 1500s, the plant had come into favor as a strong flavoring to override the saltiness of cured meat. Some also identified the plant with love or perhaps considered it an enticement to love. An alluring perfume popular with European ladies combined rosemary flowers with wine. When sugar was added to the mix, the concoction was transformed into an invigorating, cure-all drink. Perhaps this is why writers of the 1600s identified rosemary with cheerfulness. People associated rosemary with good health as late as the Victorian era (1837–1901). During that time, British gentlemen put sprigs of rosemary in the hollow handles of their walking sticks so they could sniff the contents. This practice was thought to ward off disease.

Eating Rosemary

Rosemary is a seasoning closely identified with Italian and French cooking. People often use fresh or dried rosemary leaves with poultry or lamb, in soups, and in stews. Rosemary also tastes good sprinkled on pizza and mixed into olive oil for sautéing vegetables or meats.

Rosemary is an evergreen—it keeps its green leaves all year round.

Parsley

To Your Health!

Rosemary retains its medicinal value among herbalists, who recommend the powdered leaves for depression and digestive problems. In addition a 1996 study by the American Institute for Cancer Research proved that powdered rosemary is highly effective in preventing breast cancer in laboratory rats.

Parsley

Crisp, fresh parsley is a member of the carrot family and a cousin of caraway, dill, and cumin. Parsley comes in two varieties—curly-leaf and the more flavorful flat-leaf Italian. The plant grows from a long, carrotlike root and produces multiple yellow flowers on the end of a long stalk. For the best flavor, parsley should be picked before flowers appear.

Wild parsley once grew from Mediterranean Europe across North Africa to the Middle East. Although no one knows when, experts believe that people domesticated parsley early in prehistoric times. Ancient people used parsley so frequently for healing and for cooking that they took it for granted and scarcely wrote about it. The Greeks bordered their gardens with the plant. They ate little of it, though, preferring to feed it to their horses. The ancient Romans, on the other hand, ate parsley sandwiches for breakfast and chewed parsley to relieve garlic breath. Until the 1600s, Europeans thought of parsley as good for the liver.

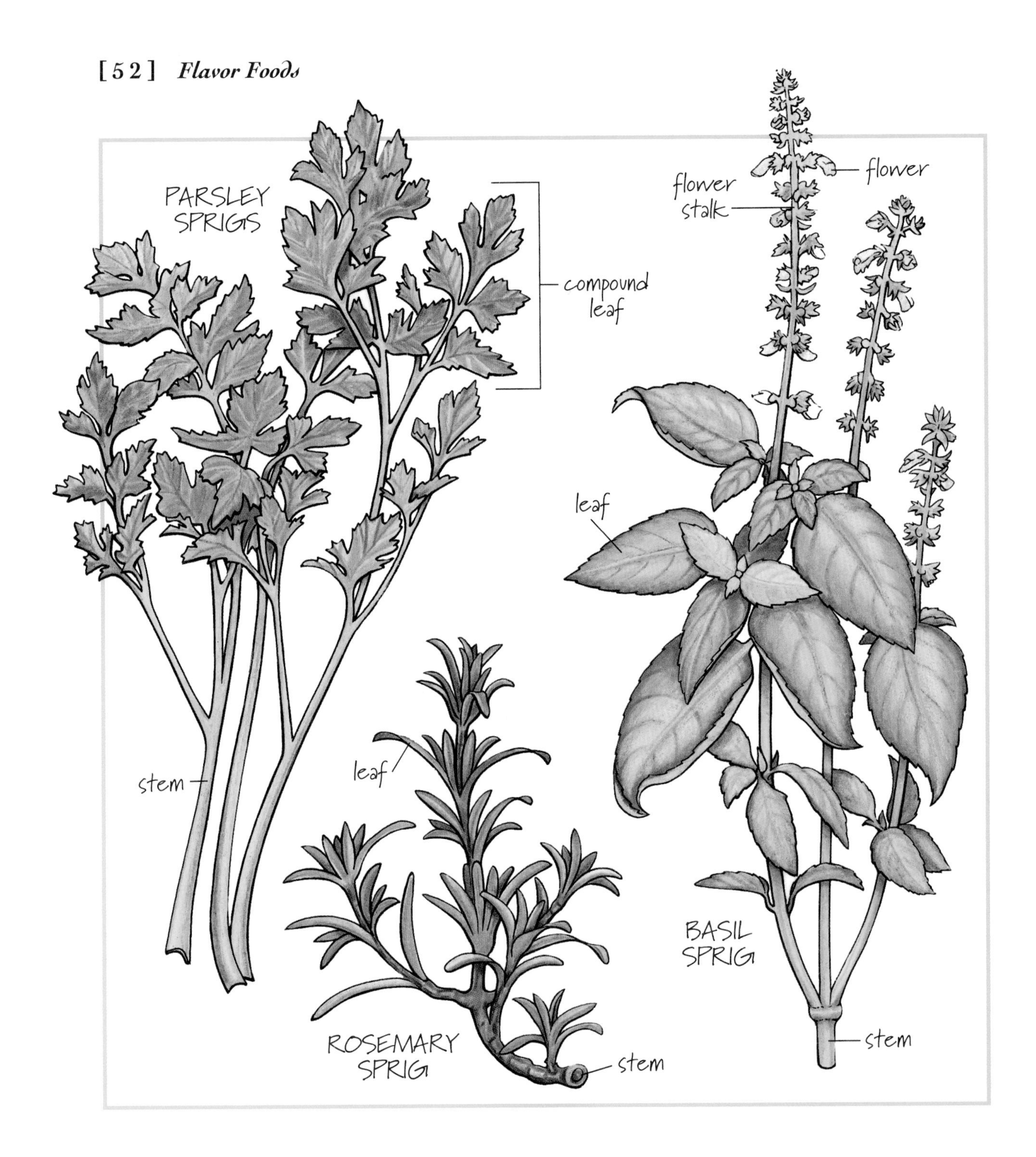
PARSLEY SPRIGS
compound leaf
stem
flower
flower stalk
leaf
BASIL SPRIG
stem
leaf
ROSEMARY SPRIG
stem

A Minnesota herb grower sells young plants to home gardeners at a street market.

Please Pass the Parsley

Europeans have long considered parsley an indispensable herb for every cook, and it was always included in any mixture of chopped fresh herbs. Two classic French herb mixes start with parsley. *Fines herbes*—often used with omelets—requires parsley, chervil, chives, and tarragon. A cook's favorite for fish, a *bouquet garni* consists of parsley, tarragon, fennel, and lemon balm. People toss the fresh or dried leaves into everything—soups, salads, stews, fish, vegetables, meats—with the possible exception of desserts.

Parsley is, of course, famous as a garnish. It's the sprig of greenery that arrives with the meal at many restaurants. Alas, parsley garnishes usually remain uneaten, even though parsley is a good source of iron, which allows the body to use oxygen, and vitamin C, important for healthy body tissues.

Growing Herbs

Most herbs thrive on sun and well-drained, fine-grained soil. Some growers raise herb seedlings in greenhouse beds and then plant the crop outdoors. Others plant outdoors from seed. A tractor pulls a device called a drill, which plants individual seeds in rows about 30 inches apart. Basil pops up within two weeks. Parsley takes a little longer. Farmhands thin (selectively pull up) the young plants to leave about 6 inches of space between them. Farmers use chemicals, machines, or good old-fashioned hoeing to control weeds. The crop receives moisture by drip irrigation—a system of hoses that provides specific amounts of water directly to the plants' roots. Rosemary needs less water than most other herbs.

Herbs to be sold fresh are always harvested by hand. Every three weeks or so, farmworkers cut the plants with scissors. They gather the crop in baskets and put it on refrigerated trucks. The trucks bring the herbs to a processing area for sorting, cleaning, and packing. The herbs go into three-ounce packs for professional chefs and one-ounce packs for the supermarket customer.

A tractor cuts a field of peppermint. The crop will be left to dry in the field for a few days before workers gather it.

Growers use machines to harvest herbs that will be sold dry. The mechanical harvesters used on large California farms can usually be adjusted to cut different kinds of herbs. The harvesters cut back the herbs halfway. Usually the herbs will respond with new growth, allowing three or four harvests of the same plants.

Trucks bring the harvested herbs to an automated processing site. Machines clean the herbs of stems and debris. Then the leaves are ready for drying. Different herbs require different methods of drying to best preserve color and flavor. The produce might be dried in plain air, over heat, or in the shade. Workers inspect the dried herbs and

Magnificent Mint Family

Peppermint *(Mentha piperita)* and spearmint *(Mentha spicata)* are the plants we think of most often as mints. But the mint family, Labiatae, includes basil and rosemary as well as marjoram, sage, savory, and thyme. Some green, some grayish green, mint plants might grow to a height of about two feet or creep low as a ground cover.

Peppermint and spearmint have long been thought to soothe upset stomachs and stop hiccups. Many people threw chopped mint leaves into their baths in the Middle Ages. They also scattered the leaves about to repel rats. Mint leaves were used to whiten teeth and to ward off headaches. These days mint is more likely to season iced tea, roast lamb, or Middle Eastern yogurt-cucumber salads. On the industrial side, spearmint and peppermint oils turn up as flavorings in toothpaste, mouthwash, candy, and chewing gum.

FINES HERBES

1 sprig fresh parsley (flat-leaf is better)
1 sprig fresh tarragon
1 sprig fresh chervil
4 or 5 fresh chive leaves

If you'd like to be an instant French cook, assemble some fines herbes (pronounced feen EHRB). The phrase means "fine herbs" and refers to a traditional mix of herbs. You can find the fresh ingredients at a farmer's market, a health food store, or at your supermarket. If you can't find fresh herbs, you can use ½ teaspoon of each kind dried, but your herb mix won't taste nearly as good.

Place the herbs on a cutting board and mince them finely with a knife. Put them in a small bowl and mix. That's it! Add fines herbes to an omelet, toss them on rice, or stir them into soup. Sprinkle them anywhere you want a burst of fresh herb flavor.

then ship them in bulk to a packer. There an automated assembly line packages the herbs in small bottles or bags for shipment to stores.

Egypt supplies 80 percent of all the basil imported into the United States. Growers also raise basil in Southeast Asia, Hungary, France, and Morocco, as well as in Florida, New York, and the cooler coastal areas of California.

Bark

[*Cinnamomum zeylanicum*—cinnamon]
[*Cinnamomum cassia*—cassia]

Bark is the outermost part of a tree. The layer called inner bark conducts food—which the leaves create by photosynthesis—from the leaves to the roots. The tough, older, outer bark seals in the tree's moisture and protects the tree from predators and diseases.

Cinnamon and Cassia

Cinnamon is the bark of tropical evergreen trees of the laurel family. In the wild, the trees grow to 60 feet or more. "True" cinnamon, also called Ceylon cinnamon, is native to Sri Lanka (formerly Ceylon), an island off the southern coast of India. Cassia, or Chinese cinnamon, grows throughout Southeast Asia. Its bark is slightly darker in color and subtly different in taste. Accounts are sometimes muddy as to which cinnamon is which, and history often lumps the two together.

Cinnamon is for lords, cassia for common people.

—John Russell

Cinnamon sticks

Cassia bark is coarser than that of true cinnamon.

The first written reference to true cinnamon came from the Chinese emperor Shen Nung in 2700 B.C. Shen Nung promoted all things agricultural, and this tree from Ceylon caught his attention. The ancient Chinese also knew cassia and considered it the Tree of Life—the centerpiece of their concept of paradise.

Cinnamon was scarce and expensive for the ancient inhabitants of Europe. Arab traders controlled its sale for centuries, marketing bark collected from wild trees. The ancient Greeks and Romans flavored their wine with cinnamon. The most famous cinnamon consumer in history was the Roman emperor Nero, who governed from A.D. 54 to 68. He murdered his wife and then made amends by ceremoniously burning her body with a year's supply of the sweet and pungent spice.

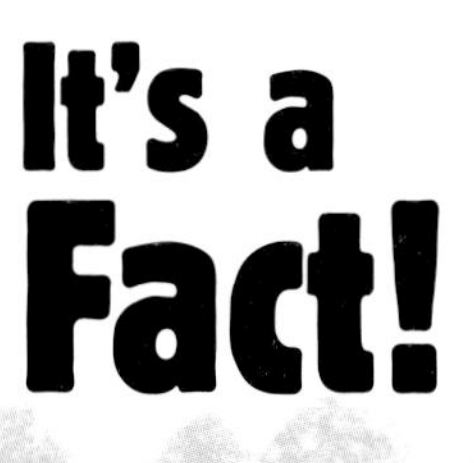

Cinnamon is an important source of oleoresins. These are concentrated flavorings, including the essential oil of the plants. Oleoresins are important in a wide range of commercial baked goods and in a surprising list of processed meats, including bologna and boiled ham. Medicines and antibacterial products also contain cinnamon extracts.

The Dutch East India Company's headquarters stood in Batavia—later Jakarta, Indonesia's capital.

With the return of the Crusaders to Europe from the Middle East, and following the journeys of Marco Polo, cinnamon became a European favorite. At first people used it to disguise the taste of spoiling meat. Soon it was a key ingredient, particularly in French, Italian, and English food.

Through the 1500s and 1600s, the Portuguese and the Dutch controlled the cinnamon trade. The Dutch East India Company earned most of its money by selling cinnamon, and in the 1700s, the Dutch were the first to successfully cultivate true cinnamon trees. But around 1770, spice bandit Pierre Poivre stole some cinnamon cuttings from the Dutch groves and brought them to French tropical colonies. The French cinnamon industry that emerged increased the global cinnamon supply and sent world prices plunging. In response the Dutch destroyed many hundreds of trees in an effort to reduce cinnamon stocks and thereby boost prices. Instead the Dutch ruined the livelihood of the people of Ceylon and their own trade. The British took over Ceylon in 1796 and dominated the cinnamon trade well into the 1800s. But by then, both cassia and true cinnamon trees had been planted from Malaysia to the Seychelles, as well as in the West Indies and Brazil. With plenty of spice sources, supplies became steady and prices decreased.

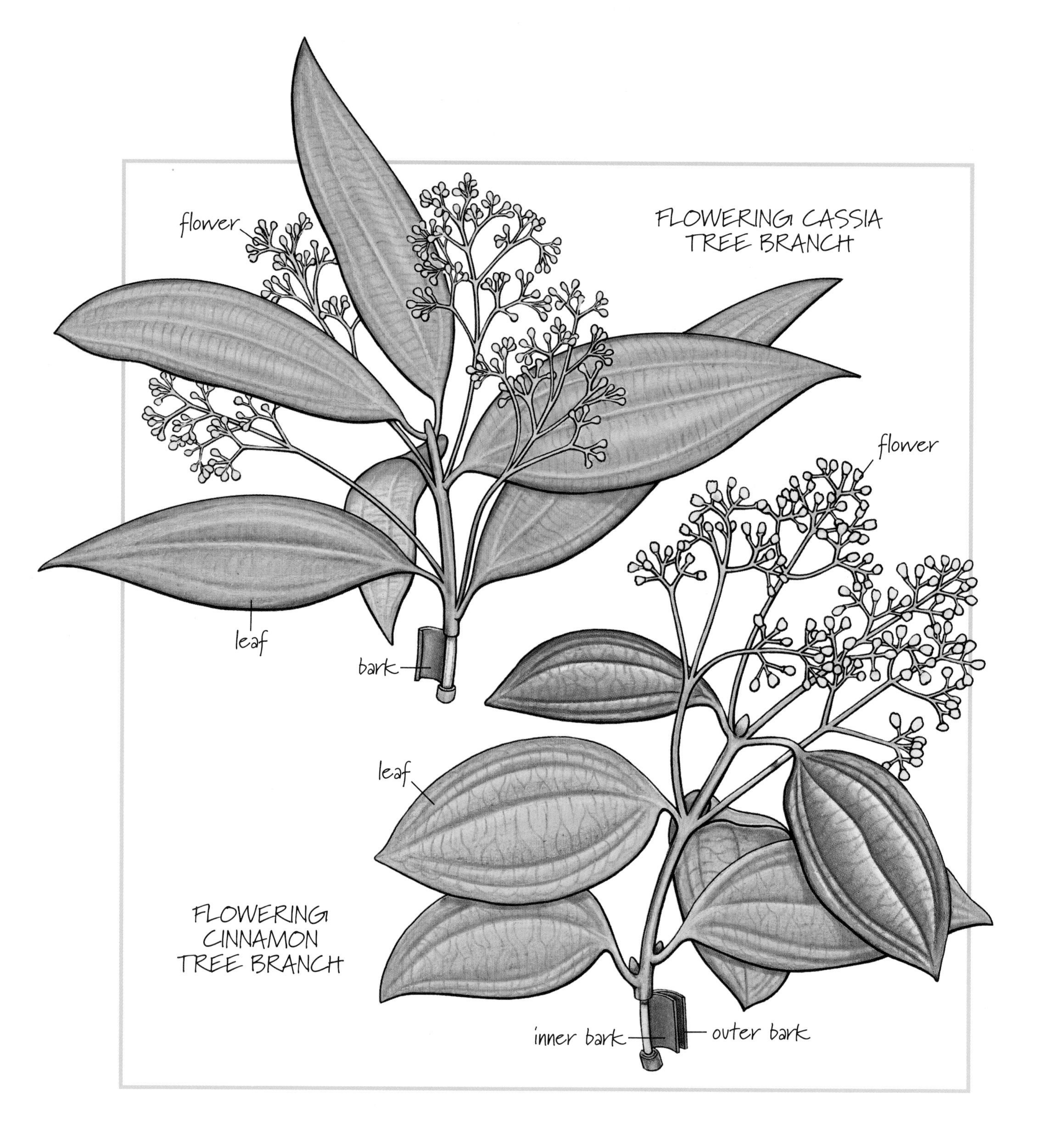
FLOWERING CASSIA
TREE BRANCH
flower
leaf
bark
flower
leaf
FLOWERING
CINNAMON
TREE BRANCH
inner bark
outer bark

An Indonesian man peels bark from the trunk of a cinnamon tree.

Growing Cinnamon and Cassia

Both cinnamon and cassia grow in warm, rainy parts of the world. True cinnamon is cultivated in Sri Lanka, southern India, Brazil, and Indonesia. Cassia is grown in Indonesia, China, Laos, Cambodia, and Vietnam. Farmers plant cinnamon trees from seed and allow them to grow for two years before the first harvest. Then farmhands cut off the tree's green shoots and peel the bark from these. The outer layer of bark is discarded, leaving strips of the inner layer. Workers leave these strips to dry slowly. True cinnamon bark curls into quills, or tight cylinders, and these are often sold as cinnamon sticks. The harvest every two years is, for the tree, a pruning. These trees usually grow only about seven feet tall. Cassia bark may come from the branches or trunk, and its outer layer need not be removed. Cassia dries in strips or chips.

Workers cut the thicker bark of trunks or main branches for use in making cinnamon extracts.

Different Tastes for Different Places

Cinnamon and cassia taste slightly different. Cassia has a strong, spicy-sweet flavor. Cinnamon tastes sweet and woody, less robust and more delicate than cassia. People in various parts of the world may or may not appreciate the subtleties between the two cinnamons. Sellers in the United States lump cassia and true cinnamon together and treat them as the same, both in statistical data and, generally, in labeling aimed at the consumer. In Britain, on the other hand, laws keep the two strictly separate. Mexicans use true cinnamon almost exclusively.

Stick It in Your Food

The flavor of cinnamon goes well with both sweet and savory foods. Baked goods, holiday drinks, and stewed fruits all benefit from a little cinnamon. Chocolate and cinnamon are frequently combined. And Mexican desserts—which are bland and sweet in contrast to the spicy main dishes—often feature the spice. Moroccans put cinnamon in stews called *tagines*. In China, where people distinguish between cinnamon and cassia, cooks often add cassia to sauces or braised dishes. Indians include cassia in pilaf, a spiced rice dish with chunks of meat or vegetables.

Noble Laurel

The "noble laurel" or bay tree, a cinnamon relative, is native to the Mediterranean. Ancient Greeks crowned their heroes with wreaths woven from laurel twigs. These days cooks add an aromatic bay leaf to soups, stew, or stocks to "crown" these dishes with a sweet, mellow flavor.

Bay leaves

Zimt und Mandelschnecken (Cinnamon-Almond Snails) (6 snails)

6 pieces of frozen dinner roll dough, thawed for 3 hours
¼ cup whole almonds
7 tablespoons butter, melted
½ cup brown sugar
1 tablespoon cinnamon

Place the pieces of dough on a floured breadboard, cover them with a dish towel (not terrycloth), and place them in a warm spot (about 180°) until the dough has doubled in size (about 2½ hours). Chop the almonds into small pieces and brown them in 1 tablespoon of the butter. Combine the browned almonds, sugar, and cinnamon and set the mix aside. Generously grease a 6-well muffin pan. Roll each piece of dough into a 4X6-inch rectangle. Using 4 tablespoons of the melted butter, brush each piece lightly. Sprinkle each piece with some of the sugar-almond-cinnamon mixture. Roll up the dough lengthwise to form 6-inch logs. Pinch the ends together, then form the logs into crescent shapes and place one in each well of the muffin pan. Brush the remaining butter on each roll. Preheat the oven to 350°.

Cover the pan with the dish towel again and let the dough rise for 15 to 20 minutes. Remove the towel and bake for 20 minutes or until the snails are lightly brown. Cool them in the pan for 5 minutes, then remove each roll from the pan and place on a cooling rack, glazed side up. Serve the cinnamon-almond snails warm for a breakfast commonly enjoyed in Austria, a nation in central Europe.

Roots and Rhizomes

[*Zingiber officinale* — ginger]
[*Glycyrrhiza glabra* — licorice]
[*Armoracia rusticana* — horseradish]
[*Curcuma longa* — turmeric]

Rhizomes are underground stems that sprout roots and shoots. Both ginger and turmeric grow from rhizomes. Horseradish and licorice, on the other hand, are roots — underground structures through which the plant draws nourishment from the soil.

Ginger

Ginger grows about three feet high and has reedlike leaves. It flourishes in the tropics but can also grow in warmer temperate zones. Ginger originated in India or Malaysia so long ago that no one can say precisely where or when. The plant's name derives from the Sanskrit word *sringavera,* meaning "horn root." The part that people eat resembles a comic-strip reindeer's antler. Botanically, however, the horn root is a rhizome.

Dried ginger roots are ready for grinding.

The herbs were springing in the vale: Green ginger plants and licorice pale . . .

— Geoffrey Chaucer

[Turmeric] has all the properties of true saffron, as well the smell as the color, and yet it is not really saffron.

— Marco Polo

. . . the Horse Radish stamped with a little vinegar put thereto . . .

— John Gerard

Ginger flowers grow on long spikes.

Hindu holy men of ancient India considered the seasoning pleasing to the gods. The ancient Chinese appreciated the flavor and medicinal power of ginger. By the 400s B.C., they were carrying pots of planted ginger on seagoing ships. Perhaps they understood the need for fresh vegetable food to combat scurvy—a disease caused by vitamin-C deficiency. The problem was once common among sailors, who spent weeks away from land with few sources of C.

The Persians of ancient Iran may have first brought ginger from India into the Mediterranean region. The spice made few waves in Greece, but the Romans received it well. As with many exotic goods, ginger from India arrived by ship in Alexandria for transport elsewhere in the empire. Romans were willing to pay high prices for their ginger, too, even though it was available in great quantities. Seeing a moneymaking opportunity, the Roman government placed heavy taxes on the spice. Wealthy Roman citizens ended up paying more for ginger than they did for the much scarcer pepper.

We know little of how the Romans cooked with ginger. The Egyptians may have passed gingerbread along to the Romans. Roman soldiers and their families carried gingerbread recipes throughout the empire. In the Middle Ages, Europeans valued ginger as a digestive aid. They cooked widely with the spice, using it powdered, chopped, grated, and sliced. By the end of the 1300s, sugar was being used to preserve ginger.

Spanish traders introduced ginger into the West Indies in the 1500s. In the middle to late 1500s, European merchants were buying ginger from the Caribbean islands of Hispaniola, Cuba, and Jamaica. English settlers on the West Indian island of Barbados were growing ginger by 1635. In the early 1600s, English settlers brought imported ginger to the east coast of North America.

During the era of Queen Elizabeth I, who ruled England from 1558 to 1603, gingerbread was in vogue. Elizabeth hired a special baker to create gingerbread likenesses of her court favorites. The baker decorated many of them with gold leaf, a custom that spread across Europe. It is said that when Peter the Great was born in Russia in 1672, his father received dozens of huge gingerbread creations from his friends, including a replica of the Kremlin, Moscow's fifteenth-century, walled-in neighborhood. Large gingerbread figures are still baked in Belgium and the Netherlands, and "gingerbread men" are well known to British and North American children.

Ginger cookies were popular in colonial Virginia in the 1700s. Political candidates passed them out, hoping that a cookie shared would mean a vote cast in their favor. Later, similar fare was part of standard rations for the Continental Army during the American Revolution (1775–1783). Ginger ice cream is still found in New England but rarely elsewhere in the United States. New Englanders also offer candied ginger as an after-dinner treat.

Growing Ginger

In Jamaica—source of the world's best ginger—small farmers usually grow the crop, doing all the labor by hand. First the growers plow their land—ginger grows best in loose, rich soil. Then workers place rhizome cuttings, along with fertilizer, about four inches apart. Ginger requires only moderate amounts of water, so irrigation is not a worry as the plant grows. Each plant may produce anywhere from two to five "hands," or large sections, of ginger. After about three to six months, the tender, young rhizomes can be dug from the ground if they're to be sold fresh. Workers wash the ginger, then dry it in the sun for a few days. At this point, the roots will keep for months if stored properly.

A boy in Nepal digs up hands of ginger in his family's farm plot.

Spice merchants unload sacks of dried ginger in Cochin, India.

If the crop is to be dried, farmers leave it in the ground for eight to ten months before harvesting, thereby allowing more flavor to develop. Growers clean and peel the ginger then dry it in the sun for about a week. The dried rhizomes are then packed into woven bags, about 50 pounds to a bag, and sent to be ground or sold whole.

Farmers in China and India produce most of the world's ginger, and growers raise the rhizome in the West Indies, Africa, Hawaii, and northern Australia, too. China, India, and most other Asian countries use plenty of fresh and dried ginger in many main course dishes, including stir-fries and curries. The Japanese pickle paper-thin slices of ginger to make two different condiments—pink *sushoga* and red *beni-shoga*. Many people around the world enjoy ginger preserved in syrup or crystallized in sugar, as a seasoning for baked goods, or in beverages such as ginger ale, ginger beer, and ginger tea.

Horseradish

Probably native to eastern Europe, horseradish is neither a horse nor a radish, but rather a member of the mustard family. In English the word *horse* can describe something large or coarse—hence *horseradish,* a large, coarse radish. The plant puts forth slender stalks that grow curly, slightly poisonous leaves up to three feet high. The large, edible root sprouts smaller, tangly side roots. If the main

Harvested horseradish roots

GINGER BEER
(3 QUARTS)

¾ cup (¼ pound) grated ginger root
2 tablespoons lime juice
½ teaspoon cream of tartar
12 cups (3 quarts) plus ¼ cup water
2 packages (¼ ounce each) active dry yeast
½ cup plus 1½ cups sugar

This refreshing, fizzy drink comes from the Caribbean country of Trinidad and Tobago, a single nation made up of two islands near the northeastern coast of South America. First, in a large bowl, combine the grated ginger root, the lime juice, and the cream of tartar. Stir well. In a large kettle, bring 12 cups of water to a boil over high heat. Carefully pour the boiling water over the ginger mixture and set the bowl aside to cool. In a small bowl, stir together the ¼ cup of water, yeast, and ½ cup of sugar to make a smooth paste. When the ginger mixture is lukewarm, add the yeast mixture and stir well. Cover the bowl loosely with plastic wrap and let it stand for three days. Then pour the ginger beer through a sieve with another large bowl underneath to catch the liquid. Add the remaining sugar and stir well. Serve chilled over ice.

root is pulled up, the side roots break off, remain in the ground, and eventually sprout up again. Woe to the home gardener who finds that horseradish has "escaped" from the tended patch to grow in the lawn. Getting rid of the tough, hardy plant is nearly impossible.

In England during the 1200s, horseradish was exclusively a medicine. People still claim a wide variety of health benefits from the plant. It has been used to relieve joint pain, to aid digestion, to maintain healthy kidneys, and to cure coughs and colds. Indeed, the root contains a chemical called allyl isothyocyanate, which gives horseradish its sharp smell and taste and is guaranteed to open anyone's stuffed nose.

The root had made the leap to the table by the 1500s. English and German diners liked horseradish sauce on their meat and fish. Grated horseradish is still popular in northern and eastern Europe.

Hot and Tasty

Horseradish is a cold-climate plant. A few farmers grow it commercially in northern California and in Illinois. Growers plant the small side roots as deep as 12 inches in rich soil. Aside from weeding, there is little else to do for this agreeable, easy-growing plant. Harvest begins in September, although some growers leave the root in the ground longer to develop its pungency.

Hot, tangy horseradish is still enjoyed on meats and fish. Shoppers can often find fresh roots in the supermarket. Many styles of prepared horseradish sauce are available as well. The freshest sauces are creamy white in color. As prepared horseradish ages, it darkens and loses some flavor.

Licorice

The word licorice and its genus name, Glycyrrhiza, come from the Greek words glycys, "sweet," and rhiza, "root."

Licorice candy used to be made exclusively from the hard, dried, yellow root of *Glycyrrhiza glabra*. A member of the pea family and native to southeastern Europe, licorice grows about four feet high. The plant has bluish purple and white flowers that resemble the blooms of the sweet pea.

Licorice has been discovered in the tombs of Egyptian pharaohs, including that of Tutankhamen, who lived from 1356 to 1339 B.C. Perhaps their subjects intended that in the afterlife, the rulers should drink *mai sus*—a sweet, licorice-flavored drink still enjoyed in Egypt. The ancient Egyptians, as well as the Greeks and Romans,

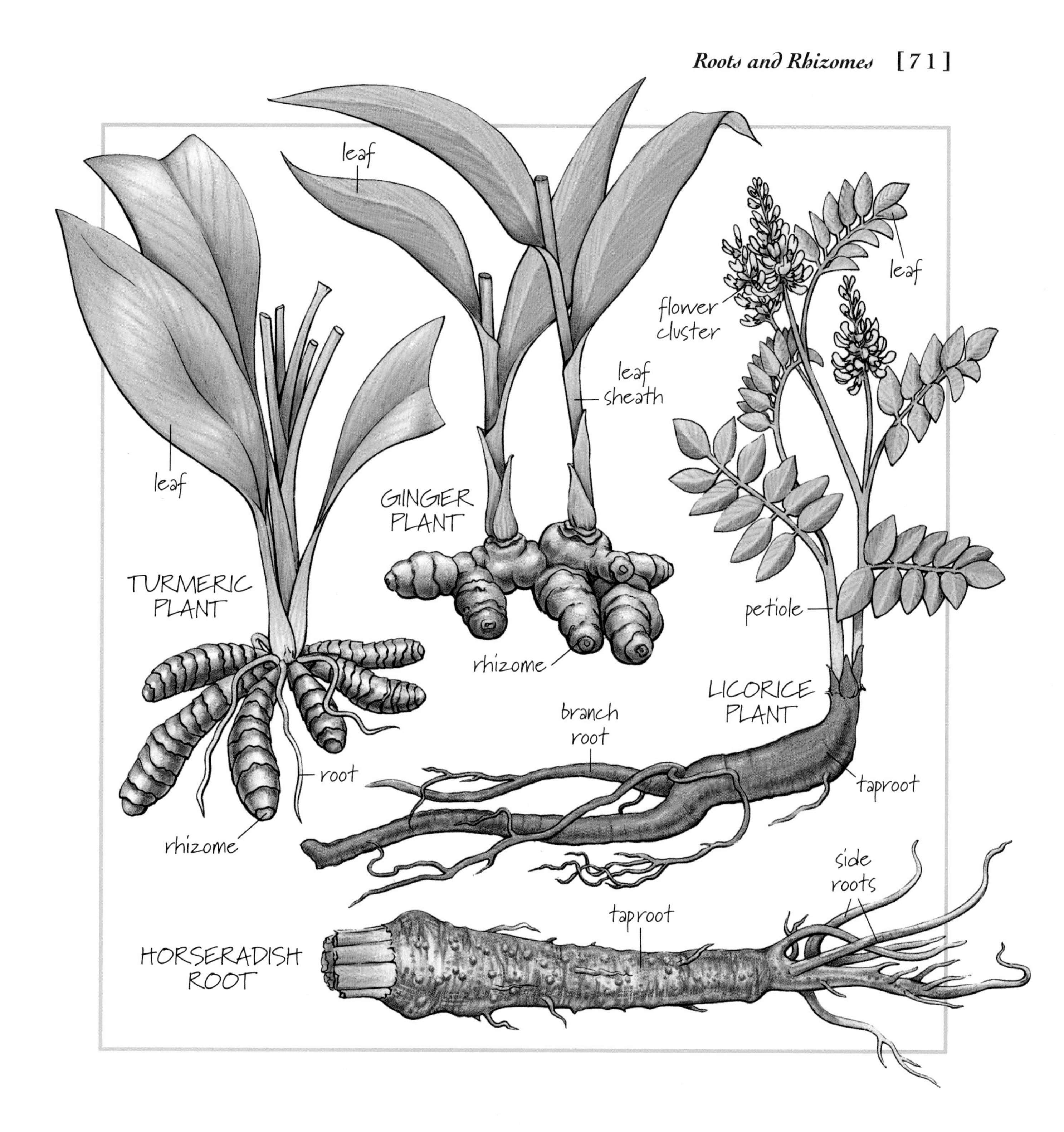
leaf
leaf
leaf
flower cluster
leaf sheath
GINGER PLANT
TURMERIC PLANT
petiole
rhizome
LICORICE PLANT
branch root
root
taproot
rhizome
side roots
taproot
HORSERADISH ROOT
leaf

used licorice as a cold and cough medicine. Ancient Indians and Chinese knew the root and believed that consuming it increased their vigor and strength.

In the A.D. 800s, the Moors grew licorice in Spain, which they occupied from 711 to 1492. In the 1500s, the plant arrived in England with Roman Catholic monks of the Dominican order. The friars established a thriving licorice industry near Pontefract Castle in northeastern England. Pontefract became known for its lush licorice fields and for its candies, called Pontefract Cakes. These days, the licorice fields of Pontefract are long gone, but the candies still produced there carry a picture of Pontefract Castle. The licorice that flavors the treats comes from Turkey. Russia, Spain, Iran, and India also produce licorice.

This licorice flower resembles a sweet pea. Both are members of the legume family.

A turmeric plant

These days licorice flavors candies, gum, and medicines that would otherwise taste awful. European cough medicines frequently contain licorice extracts. A coating made of licorice keeps pills from sticking together.

Turmeric

A cousin of ginger that's probably native to southern Asia, turmeric puts forth long-stalked leaves about three feet high. The yellowish flowers grow in clusters on a spike, much like ginger's. The rhizomes are rough and brown on the outside and deep yellow-orange on the inside. They yield the yellow powder that most people know as turmeric.

For thousands of years, Asians used turmeric mainly as a dye and as a medicine for the liver, the skin, or for general well-being. An Assyrian text dating from 600 B.C. lists the rhizome as a dye. Turmeric's rich color traditionally provided the yellow-orange color of Buddhist monks' robes. In A.D. 1280, Marco Polo noted turmeric's similarity to saffron, and medieval Europeans called the plant "Indian saffron."

Finger Planting

Turmeric is easy to grow in hot, wet climates, and so it's inexpensive. India produces the most, but China, Indonesia, Bangladesh, and countries in the Caribbean and South America also grow the rhizome. To plant turmeric, farmers place small pieces of rhizome—called fingers—in the ground. At harvesttime the entire plant must be lifted out of the ground. Growers break off the turmeric fingers from the main rhizomes. Then workers boil or steam the turmeric and dry it in ovens until it is a quarter of its original weight. Finally the outer skin is removed, and the turmeric is ready to be sold or ground.

Turmeric is an ingredient in Indian curry. Indian vegetarian dishes, especially those with beans or lentils, often contain the spice. Indian women use a paste of turmeric as a cosmetic. Many Asians and Pacific Islanders believe turmeric to have magical powers and wear it as a protective charm to ward off evil.

To Your Health!

Ginger is a preventive treatment for cardiovascular ailments and helps to reduce blood clots. Ginger and licorice both help to heal stomach ulcers.

Studies indicate that licorice may block the buildup of cholesterol, which can form a harmful layer in people's blood vessels. Licorice appears to have antiviral effects that could help people with HIV. Licorice, ginger, and turmeric extracts are anti-inflammatory—that is, they soothe swollen or irritated tissues. Research shows turmeric to lower blood cholesterol levels, boost the immune system, and suppress cancer.

Turmeric is still often used as a cheap substitute for saffron.

In many countries of Europe and the Americas, turmeric turns up as a food coloring—most notably in hot dog mustard. Cheese, soups, butter, margarine, and pickles sometimes owe their bright hues to the turmeric plant.

Seeds

[*Brassica*—mustard]
[*Myristica fragrans*—nutmeg and mace]

Seeds are the beginning of plant life. The sprouting seed sends a new plant's root down into the soil and its shoot up toward the sun. Mature plants produce seeds. Plant populations can "move" from place to place when seeds are scattered by wind, water, birds, animals, or people. Seeds ensure that a plant species will survive and flourish. Several seeds have found fame as flavorings—the most important of which is mustard. *Myristica fragrans,* the nutmeg tree, is the world's only two-in-one-seed spice plant. The tree gives us nutmeg (the seed kernel) and mace (the seed coat).

Mustard

Giving pepper a run for its money as the world's most important spice, mustard has been with us since prehistoric times. The mustard plant bears its seeds in a pod, much like beans or peas. The seeds are tiny, but they can grow into gray-green plants from 2 to 10 feet tall, heavy with yellow flowers and buzzing with bees.

His wit's as thick as Tewkesbury mustard.

—William Shakespeare

. . . [T]he mace, very red and wrapped about the rind of the nut, and inside this is the nutmeg.

—Antonio Pigafetta

Brown and white mustard seeds

A field of wild mustard grows in Britain. People sometimes serve mustard greens *(inset)*, usually of *Brassica juncea*, boiled with ham or sautéed with garlic and oil.

A species called Brassica kalber often grows wild in North America.

No one knows mustard's place of origin. Birds and wind have always spread the plant's abundant seeds across the Northern Hemisphere. Mustard—white *(Brassica alba)*, black *(B. nigra)*, and brown *(B. juncea)*—still pops up in grain fields as a weed. People have cultivated mustard since ancient times. One of the few spices available to Europeans before the Asian spice trade heated up, mustard was known throughout European settlements during the Stone Age (roughly 2.5 million to 3000 B.C.). Ancient people from India to Egypt to Rome munched mustard seeds with meat for instant seasoning.

Mustard seeds symbolized fiery potential in ancient times. In 333 B.C., Darius, the king of Persia, challenged Alexander the Great, king of Macedonia (part of modern-day Greece). Darius presented Alexander with a sack of countless sesame seeds, each seed representing a Persian soldier. Alexander's response was a much smaller sack of mustard seed. His soldiers, though fewer in number, were too hot to tangle with.

The prepared mustards we eat probably began with the Romans. They mixed grape juice, known as must, with ground seeds to form what they called *mustum ardens,* or "burning must." (The phrase eventually evolved into the English word *mustard.*) The burning sensation occurred when the yellow powder met the juice. The curious thing about mustard powder is that on its own, it has no terribly pungent taste. When mixed with a liquid, its heat emerges with a bang.

From Roman times, France has been a mustard power. The city of Dijon has been the center of the mustard scene since the 1200s. In 1634 the town became the official mustard producer of France. Only mustards that meet specific requirements are legally allowed to carry the name Dijon on their labels. In 1777 Monsieur Grey and Monsieur Poupon invented the famous Grey Poupon Dijon Mustard. They also introduced mechanization to the mustard-making business, thus freeing workers from the drudgery of hand crushing and mixing.

Britain is another mustard-loving country. In the early 1700s, a woman known to us only as Mrs. Clements sold her Durham Mustard far and wide. Another famous brand is Colman's Dry English Mustard. It was first made in 1814 by Jeremiah Colman, a miller from Norwich, England. He figured he could grind mustard seeds in his windmill as well as wheat, and soon he founded a comany. By 1866 Colman's was so popular that four trainloads of it left the factory each day. In 1973 Colman's opened a mustard shop in Norwich to mark the firm's 150th anniversary.

Make Your Own Mustard!

It's so easy you'll wonder why you never tried it before. Put two tablespoonfuls of dry mustard powder in a shallow bowl. Add cold water, just enough to make a paste. Mix slowly and let it stand at least 10 minutes. Taste. Wow! Hot stuff!

Growing Mustard

White mustard still grows wild in North Africa, the Middle East, and southern Europe. It is cultivated in many parts of the world. Brown mustard is grown commercially in the United Kingdom, Canada, and the United States. Black mustard is cultivated in Argentina, Chile, the United States, and in some European countries. Canada is the mustard seed power of the world, growing about 90 percent of all the mustard seed on the international market. Canada exports most of its mustard seed whole, to be processed in the receiving country. The United States is Canada's biggest customer.

Some 83 percent of U.S. households use mustard. Two out of three of these households prefer yellow mustard (made with white mustard seeds) to any other. The largest importers of white mustard are the United States, Denmark, Belgium, Germany, Switzerland, and Japan. Japan, South Korea, and the United Arab Emirates import the most oriental (a variety of brown) mustard.

In Canada and the United States, farmers plant the tiny mustard seeds with a tractor and a device called a seeder, which releases individual seeds at regular intervals. After about two and a half months, the mustard is ready for harvest. Large combines—harvesting machines—enter the fields. They take up the entire plant, sending the seeds into a hopper (container) on top of the combine and spitting the rest of the plant back into the field. When the hopper is full, the combine operator empties the load into a waiting truck. The truck brings the seed to a packing area. There workers clean and sort the seeds and send them to be ground or packed whole. An acre of mustard produces one ton of seed, which makes 47,600 jars of mustard.

Yellow mustard gives hot dogs zip.

Cardamom

Native to the rain forests of India and Sri Lanka, cardamom is a 6- to 15-foot-tall member of the ginger family. The plant's half-inch-long green pods contain aromatic seeds that flavor Indian spice mixes, European baked goods, and Middle Eastern coffee.

Munch on Mustard

Northern Europeans prepare black mustard to eat with traditional peasant food. Brown mustard seeds add flavor to many African and Asian dishes. In Bangladesh people cook with a hot, spicy oil pressed from mustard seeds. And anyone who has ever sampled Chinese mustard knows that these people like it hot. In India people toast brown mustard seeds to bring out a nutty flavor and use the spice to prepare food.

Nutmeg and Mace

Another important spice derived from a plant's seed is actually two spices in one—nutmeg, the seed kernel, and mace, the lacy aril (seed coat). The two spices grow on a tree native to the Molucca Islands. The trees, which can exceed 60 feet in height, are generally either male or female. That is to say, their flowers produce either pollen (male) or fruit and seeds (female)—not both, as is typical among flowering plants. The nutmeg tree is an evergreen, with glossy, egg-shaped leaves and tiny yellow blossoms that give off a distinct, spicy aroma.

Botanists use the word *imperfect* to describe a flower that is either male or female.

Arab traders probably first carried nutmeg and mace from the Moluccas around A.D. 1000, though some place the date as early as the A.D. 500s. The Arabs probably brought nutmeg and mace to the Middle East or North Africa, where the spices were accessible to European merchants.

Nutmeg and mace grow inside a peachlike fruit. People who live in nutmeg country make the fruit into a tasty jam.

This French manuscript from the 1400s shows a fanciful nutmeg tree and a merchant weighing the spice at his desk.

By the 1100s, most European cities had nutmeg. During the late Middle Ages, it was Europe's second most popular imported spice (after pepper). But it was not cheap. During the 1300s, a pound of nutmeg cost as much as a cow.

At first nutmeg and mace were used as perfume and medicine. Sweet-smelling nutmeg served as incense, too. People gradually came to use mace more and more for cooking. During the 1600s and 1700s, Europeans were so fond of this exotic sweet spice that they carried nutmegs in special silver graters, bringing them out at mealtime to grate some on their food or into their wine.

After 1656 the Dutch, who had gained control over the Moluccas, chose the islands that could be most easily defended. They then burned all the nutmeg trees on the other islands to make sure no one else could profit from the trees. Anyone caught trying to smuggle nutmeg out of the Moluccas was put to death. The Dutch also dipped all their nutmegs in lime (a caustic substance) to stop the seed from sprouting and to prevent people from planting their own trees. Pigeons, however, defied these Dutch precautions. Birds could eat nutmeg fruits, fly to another island, and leave the seeds behind in their droppings.

By 1773 Pierre Poivre had smuggled nutmegs out of the Moluccas. He planted them successfully on the island of Mauritius, breaking the Dutch monopoly on spices. The British planted nutmeg on tropical lands in their control. Thus nutmeg was growing on several West Indian islands in the early

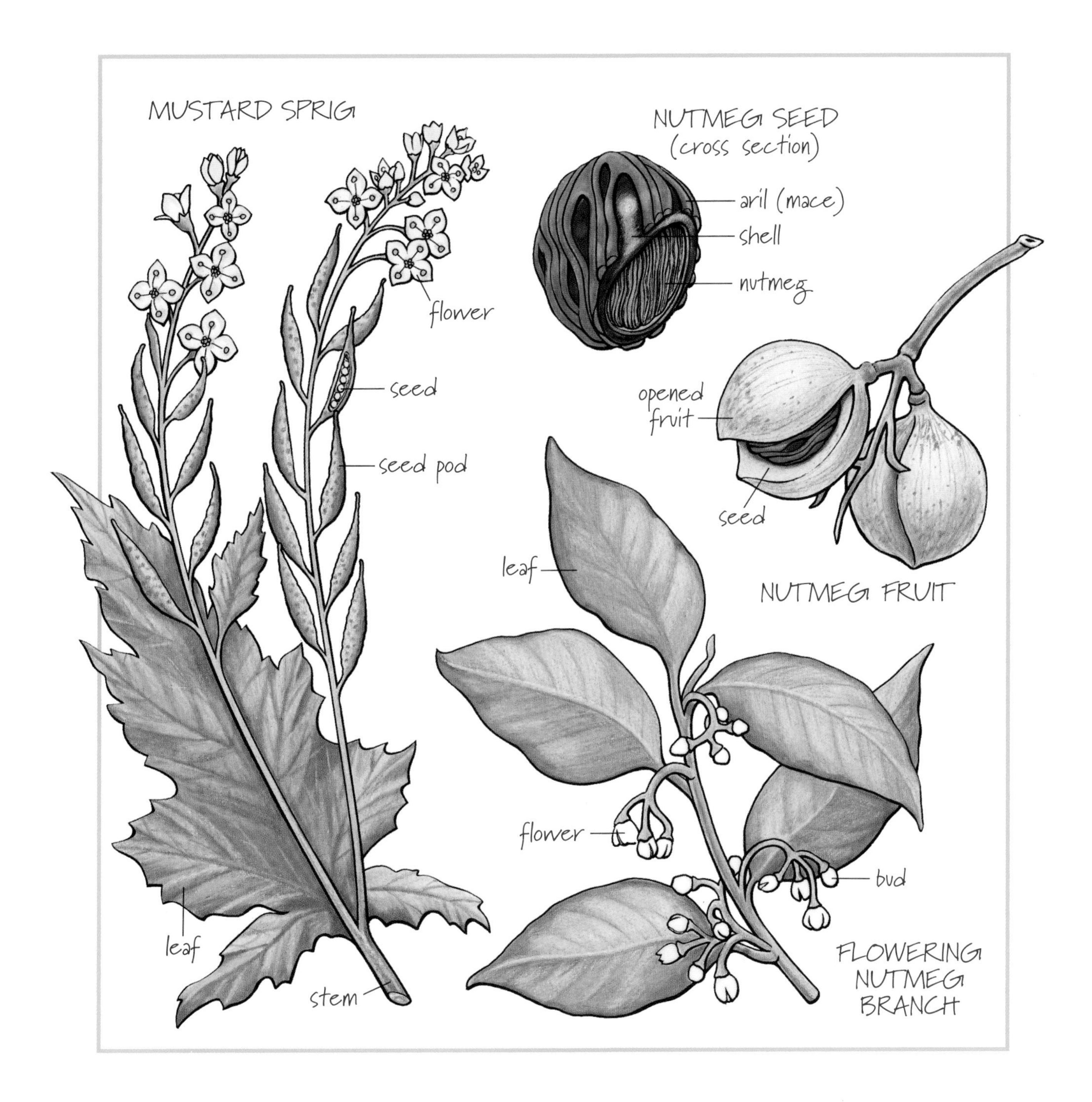
MUSTARD SPRIG
flower
seed
seed pod
leaf
stem
NUTMEG SEED
(cross section)
aril (mace)
shell
nutmeg
opened fruit
seed
NUTMEG FRUIT
leaf
flower
bud
FLOWERING NUTMEG BRANCH

A Seedy Family

Dill, caraway, and cumin all have tasty seeds and are members of the carrot family (and, incidentally, they're cousins to parsley). Fernlike, bright-green dill *(Anethum graveolens)* grows two feet high. Its tiny, white blossoms grow in wide flower heads. Russians, Hungarians, Poles, and Scandinavians are crazy about dill seed. North Americans make their pickles with it. A member of the parsley family, dill has popped up in the northern areas of Europe, Asia, and North America. Dill weed, the plant's threadlike leaves, is a must with smoked salmon. Dill and caraway *(Carum carvi)* plants look almost alike. Also a plant of the north, caraway is so old that its seeds have been found in prehistoric sites in Switzerland. Despite the plant's origins, the Arab word for the seed, *karwiya,* has given us its name. Germans, Russians, Austrians, and eastern Europeans flavor sauerkraut (pickled cabbage), cheese, dark rye breads, and all manner of stews and meat dishes with the caraway plant. They even drink extracts of the seed in the alcoholic beverage *akvavit.* Often confused with the caraway plant, cumin *(Cuminum cyminum)* has thin leaves and white or pale pink flowers. Early writers in Egypt, Greece, and Rome mentioned cumin seed, and it appears in the Bible as well. A favorite spice for making chili powder in North America, cumin also turns up in the Indian spice mixes *garam masala* and *panch phoron* and in *ras el hanout,* a spice mix from North Africa.

1800s, including Grenada by 1843. These days Grenada proudly flies a national flag featuring the nutmeg. The island nation supplies more than 40 percent of the world's nutmeg.

Growing Nutmeg and Mace

The nutmeg tree thrives best in hot, humid places. Commercial farmers grow nutmeg throughout Indonesia and in Sri Lanka, Malaysia, and the West Indies. Workers first sow nursery beds with nutmeg seeds, which sprout in about six weeks. When the young nutmeg trees are about six months old, growers transplant them to outdoor groves. To ensure plenty of fruit, 1 pollen-producing male tree is planted for every 10 fruit-bearing females. The trees grow slowly and begin producing after about 7 years. The most productive trees are between 15 and 30 years of age, although many trees live as long as 100 years.

Six to nine months after the nutmeg tree blooms, the fruit ripens and splits open to reveal the aril—the lacy, red seed covering from which mace is made. Farmhands pick the fruit at this point. Each tree yields about 10 pounds of nutmeg and close to 2 pounds of mace at each harvest. Workers remove the seed and aril from the fruit, separate the two parts, and dry them in the sun for about two weeks. The seed is shelled by machine or by hand with a wooden club. The kernel inside the seed is the nutmeg.

Food-processing companies buy spices whole and grind them into powder for sale to consumers. Mace keeps its flavor longer than most ground spices, and the tough aril is difficult to grind at home. But nutmeg loses its aroma quickly when powdered, so purists prefer to buy it whole and grate their own.

A Nose for Nutmeg and Marvelous Mace

In Southeast Asia, where nutmeg and mace originated, the two spices are used only sparingly. But in the Caribbean, a newer spice-growing area, people treat their meat with nutmeg and mace marinades or rubs and grill it up. In Europe and the Americas, people dab a bit of nutmeg on their holiday eggnog or use it to season baked goods. Cooks love fresh nutmeg in cheese dishes, cream sauces, spinach dishes, and even sausages. Nutmeg is tasty sprinkled on fresh fruits, cappuccinos, and desserts. Mace tastes similar to nutmeg and often substitutes for it. Mace is welcome in baked goods, sauces, and soups, and it's a common ingredient in hot dogs.

An Indonesian nutmeg gatherer holds his long-handled picking tool as his son shows off the day's harvest.

Chicken Curry
(4–6 servings)

½ cup vegetable oil
½ cup plus 2 tablespoons chopped onion
4 cloves garlic, peeled and minced
1 1-inch piece of ginger root, peeled and cut in half
2 teaspoons cumin seeds
4 whole cardamom seeds
1 cinnamon stick
4 whole cloves
½ teaspoon ground red pepper
1 teaspoon turmeric
6 ounces tomato paste
4 to 6 pieces chicken
2 medium white potatoes, peeled and quartered
½ cup fresh coriander

This curry comes from Ethiopia, a country in East Africa where people like things spicy. The recipe contains spices from each category covered in *Flavor Foods*.

In a large frying pan, heat the oil over medium heat for 1 minute. Add the onion, garlic, ginger root, cumin, cardamom, cinnamon stick, cloves, red pepper, and turmeric and stir. Stir in the tomato paste and cook for about 10 minutes or until the tomato paste separates from the oil. Stir the tomato paste and oil back together. Add the chicken, reduce the heat to low, and cover the pan. Simmer for 35 minutes. Add the potatoes, cover, and simmer 15 minutes or until the potatoes are tender. Add the coriander and simmer uncovered 10 minutes more. Serve.

Glossary

domestication: Taming animals or adapting plants so they can safely live with or be eaten by humans.

ornamental: A plant grown for its beauty and not for its food or commercial value.

photosynthesis: The chemical process by which green plants make energy-producing carbohydrates. The process involves the reaction of sunlight to carbon dioxide, water, and nutrients within plant tissues.

pollen: Among seed plants, the fine dust that carries the male reproductive cells. During pollination (the placement of pollen on a flower), the male cells unite with the plant's female reproductive cells (eggs), resulting in the development of seeds that can produce the next generation.

rhizome: A rootlike, underground stem.

temperate zone: A moderate climate zone that falls either between the Tropic of Cancer and the Arctic Circle in the Northern Hemisphere or between the Tropic of Capricorn and the Antarctic Circle in the Southern Hemisphere.

trellis: A framework of crossed wooden strips used to support climbing plants.

tropics: The hot, wet zone around the earth's equator between the Tropic of Cancer and the Tropic of Capricorn.

Further Reading

Barker, Albert. *The Spice Adventure.* New York: Julian Messner, 1980.

Busenberg, Bonnie. *Vanilla, Chocolate, & Strawberry: The Story of Your Favorite Flavors.* Minneapolis: Lerner Publications Company, 1994.

Fitzsimons, Cecilia. *Cereals, Nuts & Spices.* New York: Julian Messner, 1997.

Fitzsimons, Cecilia. *Vegetables & Herbs.* New York: Julian Messner, 1997.

Kite, L. Patricia. *Gardening Wizardry for Kids.* Hauppauge, NY: Barron's, 1995.

Lavine, Sigmund A. *Wonders of Herbs.* New York: Dodd, Mead, 1976.

Root, Waverley. *Food.* New York: Simon & Schuster, 1980.

Trager, James. *The Food Chronology.* New York: Henry Holt and Company, 1995.

Ready to greet her customers, a woman sells her home-grown herbs at an open-air market in India.

Index

About the Author

Meredith Sayles Hughes has been writing about food since the mid-1970s, when she and her husband, Tom Hughes, founded The Potato Museum in Brussels, Belgium. She has worked on two major exhibitions about food, one for the Smithsonian and one for the National Museum of Science and Technology in Ottawa, Ontario. Author of several articles on food history, Meredith has collaborated with Tom on a range of programs, lectures, workshops, and teacher-training sessions, as well as on *The Great Potato Book*. The Hugheses do exhibits and programs as The FOOD Museum in Albuquerque, New Mexico, where they live with their son, Gulliver.

Acknowledgments

For photographs and artwork: Steve Brosnahan, p. 5; Tennesee State Museum Collection, detail of a painting by Carlyle Urello, p. 7; © D. J. D./Dinodia Picture Agency, pp. 8, 19, 25 (bottom), 65; © Art Resource, N.Y.: Erich Lessing, pp. 10, 33; E. T. Archive/Bibliotheque Nationale, p. 12; The Granger Collection, New York, pp. 13, 14, 34, 48, 59; Hulton Getty/Liaison Agency, pp. 15, 35; Independent Picture Service, p. 21; Steve Foley/Independent Picture Service, p. 22; Holt Studios/Mary Cherry, p. 23; © Index Stock Imagery/Tom McCarthy, p. 24; © Karlene Schwartz, pp. 25 (inset), 47, 51, 76 (bottom), 79; Holt Studios/Richard Anthony, pp. 27, 67; © Nik Wheeler, pp. 28, 37, 50, 61, 78, 83; Holt Studios/Nigel Cattlin, pp. 31, 68 (bottom), 75; H. Mahidhab/Dinodia Picture Agency, p. 32 (left); Ashvin Mehta/Dinodia Picture Agency, p. 32 (right); Holt Studios/Inga Spence, pp. 36 (both), 40, 41 (bottom), 54, 57, 66; Milind A. Ketkar/Dinodia Picture Agency, p. 38; Lindt & Sprüngli (U.S.A.) Inc., p. 41(top); © Eugene Schulz, p. 42; © Wolfgang Kaehler, p. 43; © Joy Spurr/Bruce Coleman, Inc., p. 44 (top); © Adalberto Ríos Szalay/Visor, p. 44 (bottom); © September 8th Stock, Walt/Louiseann Pietrowicz, pp. 45, 55, 84; Dan Mahoney/Independent Picture Service, p. 53; Holt Studios/Bob Gibbons, pp. 58, 72 (top); Vinay Parelkar/Dinodia Picture Agency, p. 62; © Robert L. and Diane Wolfe, p. 63; © Dennis Cox, p. 68 (top); © Grace Davies, p. 72 (bottom); Holt Studios/M. Szadzuik and R. Zinck, p. 76; E. T. Archive/Biblioteca Estense Modena, p. 80; © M. Bryan Ginsberg, p. 86. Sidebar and back cover artwork by John Erste. All other artwork by Laura Westlund. Cover photo by Steve Foley.

For quoted material: p. 4, M. F. K. Fisher, *The Art of Eating* (New York: MacMillan Reference, 1990); p. 18, Thomas Ravenscroft, Song Number 7, *Deuteromelia, or the Second Part of Musicks Melodie* (London: Thomas Adams, 1609); p. 30 (top), Bruce Jay Friedman, *The Lonely Guy Cookbook* (New York: McGraw-Hill, 1976); p. 30 (bottom), as quoted by John Bartlett in *Familiar Quotations* (Boston: Little, Brown, & Co., 1901); p. 42, as quoted by Waverley Root, *Food* (New York: Simon & Schuster, 1980); p. 46, Thomas Tusser, *Five Hundred Pointes of Good Husbandrie* (London: Printed by T. R. and M. D. for the Company of Stationers, 1672); p. 56, John Russell, *Book of Nurture*, as quoted by J. O. Swahn, *The Lore of Spices: Their History and Uses around the World* (Avenel, N.J.: Crescent Books, 1991); p. 64 (top),Geoffrey Chaucer, *The Canterbury Tales* (1343?–1400); p. 64 (middle), Marco Polo, *The Book of Ser Marco Polo: The Venetian Edition* (London: J. Murray, 1921); 64 (bottom), John Gerard, *The Herball, or Generall Historie of Plantes* (London: John Norton, 1597); p. 74 (top), William Shakespeare, *Second Part of Henry IV*, act 2, scene 4; p. 74 (bottom), Antonio Pigafetta, *First around the World: A Journal of Magellan's Voyage* (New York: Harper & Row, 1964).

For recipes (some slightly adapted): p. 29, Rebecca Christian, *Cooking the Spanish Way* (Minneapolis: Lerner Publications Company, 1982); pp. 45, 55, Meredith Sayles Hughes; p. 63, Helga Hughes, *Cooking the Austrian Way* (Minneapolis: Lerner Publications Company, 1990); p. 68, Cheryl Davidson Kaufman, *Cooking the Caribbean Way* (Minneapolis: Lerner Publications Company, 1988); p. 84, Constance R. Nabwire and Bertha Vining Montgomery, *Cooking the African Way* (Minneapolis: Lerner Publications Company, 1988).